The Gift of LEADERSHIP

ANDREW BURCHFIELD

ENDORSEMENTS

"I've been involved in leading creative teams for decades, and few leaders have ever considered the art of leadership as a "gift." Andrew Burchfield has done us a great favor and opened a new door on the subject of leading and inspiring people. No matter what your title, if no one is following you, then you're not a leader. Get this book. Study it. And become the leader people need. Better yet - become the leader people want to follow."

- Phil Cooke, Ph.D. CEO of Cooke Media Group and author of *Ideas on a Deadline: How to Be Creative When the Clock is Ticking*

"*The Gift of Leadership* will motivate any level of leaders to respect the gift they have received and pass the gift to others. A needed reminder for all leaders."

- Dr. Frank Damazio, bestselling author of the leadership classic *The Making Of A Leader*

"Leadership isn't a gift for our own benefit. It's a gift to be deployed in service of others. That's the heart of this book, and I'm glad Andrew wrote it."

- Jordan Raynor, national bestselling author of *Redeeming Your Time: 7 Biblical Principles for Being Purposeful, Present, and Wildly Productive*

"What a blessing it has been to witness Pastor Andrew Burchfield over the past twenty years as he has learned, applied, taught, and grown through the leadership principles he's laid out plainly and clearly for us all in his book, *The Gift of Leadership*.

I highly encourage you to get a copy, study it, and assign it to those you mentor. His book is an excellent resource for our next generation eager for Godly examples of leadership and for the keys to becoming effective leaders themselves."

- **Brooke Asiatico, Founder and Managing Partner (Asiatico Law, PLLC)**

"Andrew Burchfield masterfully shares the importance and value of proper leadership. I have been recognized and quoted for writing books and articles on leadership around the country and internationally.

Yet, I must say that I'm refreshingly encouraged by the substantive and practical application Andrew gives to us in this well-thought-out and written book… not written from theory, but from proven principles and life experience. His years of experience and level of maturity are highlighted throughout the book.

One of my mentors used to say, "Time like light makes things manifest. Given enough time, the true character (or impact) of a man or woman is made known." Time has proven the life message and fruitful leadership of Andrew Burchfield."

- **Doug Stringer, Founder & President, Somebody Cares International**

"I've been a student of leadership for over 40 years. Andrew's book, *The Gift of Leadership*, is one of the most well-written. In this book, Andrew has addressed the specifics it takes to be a well-rounded leader.

While there are many who are who have talents and gifts, it is important to develop all of the necessary skills that go into great leadership, like family, integrity, honor, and compassion. Andrew has personally impacted our team and organization. I am confident this book will impact thousands of others.

I highly recommend this book as a personal training tool or a resource for your staff that will transport your business or organization to new levels of performance and success."

- Dr. Bill Moore, author of *4 ways to Sunday*
Senior Pastor, Livingway Family Church

"Pastor Andrew Burchfield is a gifted leader and a builder of people. I have seen, firsthand, his innovative and anointed leadership gift in operation. In his various leadership capacities, Andrew leads tens of thousands of people and does it with ease. I am so glad that he has taken the time to write *The Gift of Leadership*. This will be a huge blessing to your life."

- David Hall, Senior Pastor & Evangelist,
Revival City Church, Australia
State President, Assemblies of God, South Australia

"As one of the most innovative and prolific Leaders of our generation, Andrew Burchfield understands *The Gift of Leadership* in multiple dimensions. Over the years, I've been privileged to witness Andrew's leadership lead and launch thousands of leaders.

In my life, Andrew's gift of leadership has been paramount to the development of what God has entrusted to me. This book will not only speak to the leader you are today, but it will also speak to the leader in you that God is raising up for tomorrow. Get this book, gift this book, and review it regularly!"

- Cody Graves, Founder of
Mandate Global | UnCommon.Online

"I've had the privilege of getting to know Andrew over the past decade and am grateful for how he has spoken into my leadership in so many different ways. He has in so many ways challenged me to become a leader worth following.

This is a resource that will allow the depths of Andrew's wisdom to speak into countless leaders for years to come. Andrew is an integrous and thoughtful leader that speaks transparently from his unique experiences in leadership and opportunities to learn Biblical leadership from a diversity of other great leaders that invested into him."

- Nils Smith, Chief Strategist of Social Media
and Innovation at Dunham+Company

"I love the leadership paradigm that Andrew introduces us to in this book. He thoughtfully presents the concept of leadership as tangible and practical. This book is a refreshing reminder that leadership has more to do with building people than building brands. In a leadership famine where influence is bought and not built, Andrew does an excellent job reminding us that the future belongs to the givers. I highly recommend this read for anyone who dreams of making a difference."

- Jarrell, Hip Hop Artist and
Founder of The RISE Movement

"Leadership is a gift; in this book, Andrew Burchfield shows us how we all have the gift to lead when we lead a Godly life. The book ties together leadership and spirituality with multiple tactics for success. Andrew Burchfield does an amazing job of blending leadership and faith in one book, a must read for young adults to experienced CEOs!"

- Randall J. Hoyer, Former Columbus ISD and
Lampasas ISD School Superintendent and
Current County Judge of Lampasas County, Texas

"Andrew has put together an education in leadership in a truly remarkable way with this book. The Gift of Leadership is, at its core, a gift to potential leaders. And if you commit to the ideas and insights he shares, it will transform the intention of becoming a leader from aspirational to actual."

- Mike Vardy, author, speaker, and
productivity expert (aka The Productivityist)

"In a world crowded with leadership books, Andrew Burchfield offers a truly unique and fresh perspective on leadership. Andrew challenges that genuine leadership is not about getting others to follow you . . . but investing your life and leadership as a GIFT to help others achieve their goals and dreams. This is a must-read handbook for the beginner leader and a powerful refocusing tool for the experienced leader. This book is filled with practical wisdom and insights to inspire the new leader and challenge the experienced one. I truly enjoyed this book and admire the leader Andrew has become over the last 30 years I have had the privilege of knowing him."

- Dean Hawk, Lead Pastor of
Rock Family Church, Colorado Springs

"Andrew Burchfield is a once-in-a-generation voice. His leadership will inspire you, encourage you and cheer you on to a whole new level. Allow his book to be your guide in training and managing others to become their best."

- Debra George
Debra George Ministries, SharingJesus.online

Copyright © 2022 Andrew Burchfield.

All rights reserved. No part of this publication may be reproduced, distributed, or transmitted in any form or by any means, including photocopying, recording, or other electronic or mechanical methods, without the prior written permission of the publisher, except in the case of brief quotations embodied in critical reviews and certain other noncommercial uses permitted by copyright law. For permission requests, write to the publisher, addressed "Attention: Permissions Coordinator," at the address below.

Unless otherwise indicated, scripture is taken from the New King James Version®. Copyright © 1982 by Thomas Nelson. Used by permission. All rights reserved.

Scripture quotations marked TPT are from The Passion Translation®. Copyright © 2017, 2018, 2020 by Passion & Fire Ministries, Inc. Used by permission. All rights reserved. ThePassionTranslation.com.

All Scripture quotations are taken from THE MESSAGE, copyright © 1993, 2002, 2018 by Eugene H. Peterson. Used by permission of NavPress, represented by Tyndale House Publishers. All rights reserved.

ISBN: 978-1-7376641-4-7 (Hardback)

ISBN: 978-1-7376641-5-4 (Paperback)

ISBN: 978-1-7376641-6-1 (E-book)

ISBN: 978-1-7376641-7-8 (Audio)

Any references to historical events, real people, or real places may have been adjusted by the author to protect identities and situations.

Front cover image by Chris Perry Design.

Book interior formatting by Ben Wolf

Printed by New Creation Network, LLC., in the United States of America.

New Creation Network

1423 CR 101,

Columbus, Texas 78934

First printing edition 2022.

To my Amanda, my wife:

*You are my gift from God. A true woman of wonder.
You took the fast track and turned it into a slow stroll in the park.
You will forever be a gift to my leadership.*

CONTENTS

Leadership is a Life Thing   1
Introduction

PART ONE
LEADERSHIP | THE GIFTING

1. The Toolbox   11
   Core Principles of Great Leaders
2. Vision   15
   Vision Sees the Invisible
3. Faith   21
   Believes in the Impossible
4. Integrity   25
   Integrity is the Main Ingredient
5. Family   29
   Foundation of True Success
6. Compassion   35
   Caring About People
7. Honor   39
   Honor in 3D
8. Administration   43
   Plan on Purpose
9. Excellence   47
   An Expression of Expectations
10. The Invitation   51
    Accepting the Assignment of Leadership

PART TWO
THE LEADER | THE GIVER

11. The Journey   61
    Moments and Milestones That Make Us
12. The Promise   69
    Dreaming & Leading into the Possible
13. Leading Yourself   79
    Secrets & Systems to Streamline Life

14. Vision Vertigo 89
Balance, Boundaries, and Buddies

15. Types & Typos 99
Crafting and Creating Your Personal Leadership Identity

16. Legacy Starts Today 109
Five Behaviors Great Leaders Do Daily

17. F.A.C.T.S. 119
Building the Team

18. Mantels & Missions 133
Building Teams to Accomplish Amazing Things

PART THREE
LEADING | THE GIFTS

19. Decisions 145
Dominos and Puzzles

20. Consistency 151
Staying in Tune with the Truth

21. Time 161
You Manage Time: It Does not Manage You

22. Opportunity 173
Open Doors Leads to Open Roads

23. Pace 185
The Powerful Speed of Slow

Wi-Fi Leadership | Staying Connected to The Purpose 193
Conclusion

Notes 201
Acknowledgments 205
About the Author 207

LEADERSHIP IS A LIFE THING
INTRODUCTION

Leadership is a gift. Great leaders give you *gifts*. Leadership is given to every society, culture, and people group around the world. From parenting to police officers, pastors, and politicians, leadership is placed in our lives everywhere we go. To have a great leader is like receiving a great gift.

At some point, you will realize there were people throughout your life who helped you get to where you are today. Those people are leaders.

Maybe it was a parent, coach, youth pastor, or Sunday school teacher. Perhaps it was the manager of the night shift at your first job or the uncle you only saw three times a year. These people hold special places in our hearts and lives because of what they left to us. They left a deposit of significance, never a withdrawal for selfish gain. Thinking about it now, it may be a surprise to you how much of an impact they truly made on your life.

*The **gift of leadership** is embracing the gift a leader has given to you and using it to benefit others.*

What I believe people tend to misunderstand about leadership is its overall place in life. In every sphere of life, you see the deep need for leadership. Families need leadership to guide the day-to-day necessities of life. Marriages need leadership to remain together and in covenant.

Companies need leadership to motivate team members to hit the right marks of purpose and profit. The military needs leadership to keep soldiers safe and strategic. The government utilizes leadership to represent the needs of the people and respond to threats against their livelihoods. In religious and academic environments, leadership finds its place by educating people and extracting greatness from their lives. More than ever, true leadership is needed.

My fear is that we do not honor leadership anymore. Because the term *leader* has been equally connected to the people who've abused the title, been crushed by the pressure of performance, and mismanaged the responsibility of what it truly means to be a leader, the vast population doesn't view leadership as something to be honored and respected anymore.

Students in classrooms talk back to teachers. Streets are vandalized as the police are mocked and ignored. Husbands and wives do not respect each other, causing children to grow up with a tilted perspective of what it means to truly give your life to someone. People in the pews question those in the pulpit, while employees feel neglected by employers who would rather make a buck than invest in the team.

Leadership is not *what* you build but rather *who* you build. Jesus showed us that by developing the disciples. When we allow leadership to take its intended place in our lives, areas that seem chaotic will quickly become calm. Questions are connected to answers, and doubt is filled with certainty. Leadership is about people more than it is about the process.

You know you've encountered a great leader when you are full of gratitude, knowing your life has been impacted, and you are inspired to go do the same for someone else. Leadership is having someone help you through life and, in return, doing the same for someone else. You do not find leadership: leadership finds you when you are willing to accept the responsibility.

I believe everyone can be a leader. The journey we are about to embark on together through the pages of this book is the process of accepting the gift of leadership in your life. I realize that everyone reading this book today comes from different places and different backgrounds. I write from a place where my faith is my central core: everything in my life revolves around Jesus.

LEADERSHIP IS NOT WHAT YOU BUILD BUT RATHER WHO YOU BUILD.

Where I understand not everyone currently would subscribe to my position that Jesus Christ is Lord of all, that's what I love about leadership. It transcends your story and your beliefs and, when done correctly, just keeps giving.

During our time together, I will pull from my faith and belief in Jesus to highlight some of the lessons of leadership I have learned.

This book has been organized into three parts:

- Part 1 is about **Leadership** | The invitation and impartation of the *gifting* to lead.

- Part 2 is about **Leaders** | The development of the *giver,* and how to develop others.

- Part 3 is about **Leading** | The motivation and management of *gifts* needed to lead a vision daily.

As we start down this path together, let's make sure we have a few vocabulary distinctions figured out before we take off. Throughout this book, you will see the terms *leadership, leaders,* and *leading*.

- **Leadership** is the gifting, principle, assignment, and anointing that drives an individual toward a specific mission and vision.

- A **leader** is an individual who is willing to accept the terms and conditions of what comes with the responsibility and weight that leadership brings. A leader is not gender specific. There are great male leaders and great female leaders. For simplicity, in these writings, I will simply refer to both genders as "leaders."

- **Leading** is the decision to devote your time and resources to develop the talents within someone else and build a purpose-driven vision for the benefit of others.

The words in this book are a collection of leadership lessons, ideas, thoughts, experiences, and memorable moments from some of the greatest leaders around. My hope is that you would be open to seeing what I have seen: great leadership for what it truly is. These pages are about appreciating the lessons from the people we learn from and using the principles they have given us to "gift" generations of leaders after us.

Great leadership uses principles and responsibilities to give and grow a person through a specific season of their life so they can become the next best version of who they are destined to be. Leadership is always leaning in the direction of growth. It is the ultimate gift that will always return dividends back to you. Leadership leads the way to a new way of living. It is the gift that will always keep giving.

My wife, Amanda, loves Christmas. She's one of those people who would love for it to be Christmas time year-round if it were possible. And even though we live in Texas, where "winter" is anything below 60 degrees, there's no stopping my sweet Amanda when it comes to her holiday decor, traditional Christmas carols, and a never-ending supply of food and Christmas treats in the kitchen. As if "Christmas in July" wasn't enough, we have Christmas all the time and in so many ways. Though not everyone looks forward to it, the traditional Christmas gift exchange can be a special time when we give something to someone else that reflects our heart for them. It is chosen specifically for that person, beautifully wrapped, and will (hopefully) be enjoyed for years to come. Gifts can be a special bridge of connection between two people.

What a perfect picture of what great leadership looks like. It is a gift to someone's life that will be cherished and carried with them for years to come; and then one day, given to someone else to do the same. With that said, let's begin to unwrap this precious gift—the gift of leadership.

Part One
Leadership | The Gifting

Leadership is *spiritual*.

A position that comes with an anointing for an assignment is available to everyone who accepts it. Why is your leadership spiritual? Throughout Scripture, our loving Father is giving. John 3:16 says, "For God so loved the world that He *gave*...." When you have a gift, you give it. Where there is giving, there is leadership; and it is this gift of spiritual leadership that equips you for life and your own involvement in the kingdom of God. Ephesians 4 teaches us that for the equipping of the saints, He gave gifts.

God knows that the best model to distribute gifts to His saints is through the supernatural gifting of leadership. Like an apprentice learning a skill set from a master, leadership guides you through the seasons of your life and helps you discover who you are destined to be.

Leadership is *significant*.

Equipped for the task, leadership places you in a significant space that allows you to create and leave a lasting impact on the most important thing in the world—a person's life. A thing that has value serves a purpose. Leadership is valuable to the outcome of an individual's life. I know that even right now, you can think of the people that have stepped into your life and have helped shape who you are as a person or professional.

What would your life look like without their involvement in your life? How would things be different? The role of leadership in our lives is paramount to the trajectory and destiny we ultimately achieve.

While you were growing up, maybe you knew leadership as the person in charge or the person who called all the shots. I'd like to challenge that perspective. Leadership is not only a position or a person. Leadership is an invitation to invest yourself in the development of someone else.

LEADERSHIP IS AN INVITATION TO INVEST YOURSELF IN THE DEVELOPMENT OF SOMEONE ELSE.

Leadership isn't easy, and it is not always fun. It comes with real responsibilities, and you're not always the popular one. Leadership isn't climbing a ladder for success; it is landscaping to see what you can plant in the lives of others. Too many people are trying to turn leadership into a destination to be the keynote speaker at some trendy conference that won't be around in a decade… I want to see leaders who will invest that same energy and passion into developing the people entrusted to them, multiply their influence by stepping aside, and guiding others as they grow.

That's great leadership. Great leadership plants seeds, pulls weeds and protects the fruit. Fake leaders fake their fruit, ignore the weeds, and steal the seeds from other people's trees.

I'm not against influence. I would rather simply influence the influencers because then it is not solely about what my leadership accomplished; it is about what our leadership accomplished *together*.

Leadership holds the vision together, and principles hold leadership together. The spiritual gifting and purpose-driven significance found in leadership are displayed through daily principles. All that's needed to receive this supernatural gifting is someone brave enough to look past themselves and *accept the invitation* to be a leader.

GREAT LEADERSHIP PLANTS SEEDS, PULLS WEEDS AND PROTECTS THE FRUIT.

CHAPTER 1
THE TOOLBOX
CORE PRINCIPLES OF GREAT LEADERS

I've never known anyone to build anything without tools, and the role of the leader is no different. Leadership requires a set of tools that are entrusted to you for the purpose of accomplishing the vision and mission at hand. Over time these tools will not only mold and shape what you're leading, but they'll shape you as a leader as well. The tools we are talking about are unchanging principles. A principle is a foundation upon which we build truth. It guides our beliefs, actions, and choices day by day, seemingly unknowingly to us. It is like the first layer of Legos on the ground. It may come across as pointless, but what can be built upon that pad of possibility is truly unimaginable. By definition, a principle is: *"A fundamental truth or proposition that serves as the foundation for a system of belief or behavior or for a chain of reasoning."*[1]

We must understand the truth-giving principles applied to this life-giving assignment we call leadership. Like diamonds that are made up of many facets, leadership is made up of many different principles. Most principles spring from a deep conviction around a matter or topic, but leadership was created before all creation. God the Father knew that leadership would occupy a fundamental position in the life of a person.

Most leaders think that they are building a vision; but in reality, it is the vision that's building the leader. A part of accepting the call of leadership is accepting the pace and the path that comes with it. If you think and hear the word leadership and instantly think of 1.8 million followers on your socials and becoming a household name with a book on the best sellers list, then you have missed what the call was about altogether. The path of leadership is a path that makes you a student as much as it does a teacher. It winds you in and around the areas of life that makes a pit stop at your soul, checks your heart, and causes your brain to work overtime on the seemingly unimportant and simple things. You've heard it said, "Overnight success takes twenty years." I promise with all that success comes a path that causes deep discussions and constant character checks to make sure you are ready to handle the most important thing in any leadership assignment: people. Every leader has an invisible list of principles that make them the leader they are. Yes, things like charisma and confidence are important qualities to have, but they aren't principles. The tools we talk about today won't be your average hammer and screwdriver. We are going to dig a bit deeper into the box to talk about the principles behind the positive personality traits required for truly skilled leadership. Sometimes these tools require training, but they guarantee the best out of you and your leadership work every time. Every master craftsman shows up with their tools, and these are some areas that I think apply to us all.

What you see will change. How you perceive the world will change. Why? Because leadership comes with a responsibility—one that not everyone accepts. When you accept this responsibility, it is no longer about you, but rather about the people around you. People trust leaders to lead them to better. People need leaders to help them take the next step. People wake up hoping that there is someone they can model their life after and someone who will make a mark on them that requires a response of positive action.

The position of leadership is a sacred spot that you should not take lightly. Your leadership should humble you. It should cause you to sit back and think about the reality that people are leaning on your words, your wisdom, guidance, input, perspective, anointing, integrity, and character to help them get to the next level in life. They desire more. They desire better, and they look at us and think, "You can help me get there!" They trust that we can help not only them but their families, too. They trust us with their future! Leadership is not for the faint of heart. It is a war cry against being average, and it demands devotion and dedication to develop what's already inside of you. Leadership is a long path that will lead you straight to your daily purpose. The world needs great leaders. The kingdom relies upon great leaders: leaders who care more about their community than their career. Leaders who are willing to make the connection that causes a change in a person's life. The kind of leadership that calls you to crucify your ego and personal ambitions and serve the people entrusted to you. To think that Jesus would trust us to represent Him is a weight that we shouldn't lift lightly. It is an honor to be chosen for such a time as this.

As we navigate the next few chapters surrounding some of

the principles that make up leadership, I want you to realize that many of these principles are ones you already understand and agree with, making you a great candidate for leadership. We begin with *vision*, *faith*, and *integrity* by showing the DNA of your leadership and why these invisible principles make such a visible difference. You will see how your *family*, *compassion*, and *honor* determine the direction of your leadership decisions. Finally, you will explore the importance of *administration* and *excellence* in the experience that people have with your leadership. With that said, let us pack up our tool bag for our leadership job ahead, one principle at a time.

CHAPTER 2
VISION
VISION SEES THE INVISIBLE

Vision is seeing the end before the beginning.

Leadership requires you to have a vision for the assignment you are called to complete. It comes from the depths of your heart and makes its way to your mind through ideas and inspiration. Once we receive it, we can then complete it. How do we receive vision? It starts by hearing the voice of God for a place or a people. Occasionally, vision shows up through frustration. Do not ignore your frustration. Sometimes what frustrates you most is what you are called to correct. The frustration you face today could become your life's fulfillment tomorrow. When you have the answer to the problem, you have a vision. While that may seem intimidating, you are simply expressing the heart of God for the people in that area. Leadership is being completely, 100 percent responsible for having a vision for every aspect of the assignment. Vision will be easier to see when you denounce your ego, imagine the unthinkable, reach out with risky faith, and find what solves a problem people have.

Feed the Hungry has the vision to feed people without food. Do you believe that aligns with the heart of God? Absolutely! Compassion International wants to find loving and godly homes for orphans. Is that the kingdom? Without a doubt! I could go on and on with examples of how the heart of God is seen in the world today. However, what we see today—I guarantee—started simply as a vision. You do not see it with your natural eyes at first, but through faith and with some patience, you will obtain a promise and see the vision (Hebrews 6:11-12).

Will Mancini taught about what he calls the "vision frame."[2] Imagine a beautiful picture but no frame to go with it. If the focus is on vision, each side of the invisible frame is what holds your vision together. You need this frame for people to truly understand what you are doing and where you are going. The four sides are mission, strategy, measures, and values. Each is equally important to see the vision come to life. Let's define each a bit deeper.

Mission is what we are doing today. Vision is where we are going tomorrow. Mission and vision are consistently confused, but you can't have one without the other. It is a coin with two sides. One side is the mission, and the other is vision, but they are both needed to add value to your leadership. Suppose my mission is to jog every morning. My vision is thirty pounds lighter by summer. When you have a mission, you have a reason to wake up every day and make a difference in the world. Your mission always comes with an automatic side of passion and drive. You are excited about putting your hand to something that matters! My grandpa used to say, "Find something you love to do, and you'll never work a day in your life." That's the life of mission: doing what you love and loving what you do.

Strategy is the map of your vision. It connects the days to your destiny. It is a plan and the instructions you take to make that plan productive, like an old school road trip that did not have GPS as an option and required a folded paper map. Strategy sets out a course for how mission becomes vision over time. I don't think anyone has done this better in the business world than Elon Musk. Elon has the vision to colonize the planet Mars. However, to live on Mars, you need vehicles that run off batteries (Tesla), a way to make payments and share currency (PayPal), internet to talk to all your friends back on Earth (Starlink), and reusable rockets to make travel to the planet easier and efficient. (Space X). Elon has had major significant roles in each of those companies. Why? It's a part of his strategy that is going to help him achieve his vision. Strategy is a plan with a purpose that helps you get closer to your vision.

> **MISSION IS WHAT WE ARE DOING TODAY. VISION IS WHERE WE ARE GOING TOMORROW.**

Measures show you the progress of your mission on the way towards your vision. They are the milestones on that map that help you know where you are and when it is time to get a new strategy. It is the weekly weigh-in that confirms you have lost five pounds of your goal of thirty or the loose jeans that you can fit in again. They are moments along the way that show you your vision is being achieved. Having these measures for yourself and for the team around you is a requirement if you want to see momentum take off. Start small, and like a snowball rolling down the hill, it will get larger and make a bigger impact on your vision.

Values are anchors to your vision, constantly subconsciously guiding your daily decisions. As Craig Groeschel teaches, "Values drive what you do." You brush your teeth and shower daily because you value being clean. When you have a collective set of values that others can subscribe to, you reinforce your vision with strength. Finding what you value can be challenging at first. Focus on one word and then build short statements with those words. Here at Burchfield Ministries International, some of our words include love, faith, and the power of the Holy Spirit. Let me give you an example.

Value	Love
Memorable Phrase	Lead with Love
Included in the "Vision Guide" given to every new team member	We are leaders, and through our actions, beliefs, and conduct, we strive to represent the heart of the Father in love. With every conversation and through every confrontation, we will lead with love because we love everybody.

Values are like vitamins to a vision. You need to review them often, and it will keep your vision strong and healthy. My favorite part about strong values is it helps you when it's time to make tough decisions. Leadership is full of decisions and when you do not know what to do, look to your values for the cue on the next step you should take.

Vision comes with leadership. It is a part of the package, and it is a process! Habakkuk 2:2 instructs leaders to write the vision down and make it plain so that others can run with it. Writing it down and making it plain can take some time. Don't rush it: treat it like a big download from Heaven. The larger the download, the longer it takes. Understanding and processing vision is like playing a game of telephone with God where everyone is whispering what they heard to the next person in line, and you are the first one to hear the message. After you receive the vision, you are ready to invite others to join you in making your vision a reality.

Vision is always bigger than you. It includes a crew of people to achieve greatness. God will give you a vision; sometimes he will have you develop it with other great leaders. Your vision will serve as the primary principle of your leadership. Learn how to utilize the power it has to change circumstances, create opportunities, and make a difference in your world. Jesus said, *"Anything is possible when you believe."* (Mark 9:23) Once you have a vision, then you have faith to go with it—the second tool in your leadership toolbox.

CHAPTER 3
FAITH
BELIEVES IN THE IMPOSSIBLE

Faith is the fuel to our vision. It is the ability to believe in the impossible that drives us to go for it and see it actually take place. People can have faith in all kinds of things, and it is remarkable the silly things we see people believe in these days.

My faith is the cornerstone of not only my life but my leadership as well, and I've seen countless times what happens when you *put your faith in something:* "Now faith is the evidence of things hoped for, the evidence of things not seen" (Hebrews 11:1).

Your leadership will ignite faith in you. We use the principle of faith every single day. When you sit down on a chair with four legs, you have faith that it is going to hold you up. When you get into a car, you have faith that the vehicle is going to get you where you want to go and that all the other crazies on the road are going to play by the driving rules, too, so you can get there safely. People place their faith in things, but leadership places its faith in you.

You must believe in yourself and believe that the principles of leadership are going to drive your decisions, guide you to the right goals, and pull out the right things in people. If you do not have faith, you do not have anything. It is the foundation of leadership.

FAITH IS THE FUEL TO OUR VISION.

There's an old movie, *John Q*, starring Denzel Washington. In the movie, this normal, down-to-earth father takes matters into his own hands when his dying son needs a heart transplant, and the obstacles keep stacking up. In this highly emotional, suspenseful, and captivating story, there's a scene where a hostage negotiator, played by Robert Duvall, is trying to calm this raging father down and keep him from hurting the people in the hospital lobby that he's taken hostage. He speaks to Denzel's character and says, "You have to have a little faith, John!"

"How am I supposed to have faith when my son is dying, and there are no answers?" Denzel's character retorts.

"Because that's what faith is, John: believing when you have every reason not to," the negotiator implores.

Leadership demands belief in something and someone. You must believe that what you are setting out to do can be done. If you don't believe in what you are doing, no one else will believe either. Many times our leadership will require us to choose faith over the facts we see. You might have someone on the team who, by the performance review, should be terminated, but something in you believes there's more there, and they deserve mercy and a second chance.

Go with your gut! Tune the technicality out and trust that faith is the finish line for your leadership. Just when you think it is over or something is going to fall through, faith steps up to the plate and gives you a grand slam to lead with. One thing I know to be true is this: the Holy Spirit knows everything, and the Holy Spirit is always right. We will never let a system disrupt, discourage, or distract from what Jesus is doing in a person's life or leadership.

PEOPLE PLACE THEIR FAITH IN THINGS, BUT LEADERSHIP PLACES ITS FAITH IN YOU.

CHAPTER 4
INTEGRITY
INTEGRITY IS THE MAIN INGREDIENT

*It is not about what you are doing;
it is about who you are becoming.*

As a guide to daily decisions, leaders understand the right choice is the only choice in everything we do. It is hard to believe that people sometimes don't see the value in doing the right thing: treating people right, honoring your word, telling the truth, and taking responsibility when they make mistakes.

I was raised in a way that your highest commodity of value was your word. Your word is your bond. If you say you are going to do something, you did it. Period. Integrity is the glue that holds your life together. I heard Rick Warren give a message one time where he talked about how the word integrity comes from the word integer, a math word meaning whole. To have integrity means you are a whole person. No side deals. No two-faced leading. No hypocrisy in what you say and what you do. I like to teach our teams that *integrity is the main ingredient* of your life.

> IT IS NOT ABOUT WHAT YOU ARE DOING; IT IS ABOUT WHO YOU ARE BECOMING.

My brother and I, in our adventurous and semi-mischievous teenage years, thought it would be interesting to adjust the recipe to some sugar cookies we were attempting to bake on a weekend our mother was out of town. Through the laughs and late-night delusion, we added a full can of a popular energy drink into the unbaked cookie dough. It was awful. Some things should just not be added to the recipe. The same is true with leadership: adding in personal gain or selfish desires never tastes good in leadership.

Integrity is the main ingredient that will keep your leadership whole and be a lighthouse of example to other leaders watching you.

When you as a leader accept the importance of integrity beforehand, it is a pre-decision that has already been made for everything that comes up going forward. Integrity may require you to give a refund to a customer due to a team member's error, or work a double shift because you made a mistake on the schedule. I promise you this, though: you will never lose sleep over doing the right thing.

Pastor Rick went on to tell the story of how the *Titanic* sank in 1912. Years after the mighty vessel sank to the bottom of the Atlantic, some historians and engineers have posited that had the ship not had compartments in its hull, many more people may have survived the collision with the iceberg. You see, the ship's hull was split into tiny compartments that trapped the water flooding the ship at one end. Like a seesaw with only one rider, the ship began to lift out of the water at the opposite end. Had there been no compartments at the bottom of the ship, the water would have simply flowed throughout the ship, allowing it to stay afloat longer and buying more time for rescue crews to arrive.

Because the ship lacked integrity, oneness, and wholeness, it sank more quickly than it should have. So it is with our leadership.

Leadership is a calling that infiltrates every part of your life. A person who has to hide parts of their life from their team, friends, or even their spouse lacks integrity and doesn't deserve the honor of being called a leader. Let me give you some examples. Running the church's finances out of your personal checking account: that's not integrity. Firing a loyal member of the team to make space for a deadbeat relative: that's not integrity. Avoiding a conversation of conflict that you know needs to happen just to "keep the peace" and not rock the boat: that's not integrity.

This doesn't mean that leadership makes you perfect or that you won't go through challenges in your life or make mistakes you aren't proud of. We've all done that! It simply means that when those problems arise, you won't ignore the problem, but rather you will do the right thing and allow integrity to walk you down the path of help and healing, so you do not "sink" your life.

Mother Theresa, the great missionary to the slums of India, was asked one time how she was able to stay so focused on her life work for so long without scandal. Her simple response was,

"Spend an hour every day adoring Jesus, and then do not do what you know is wrong."[3]

Integrity is the main ingredient of leadership because it will keep you honest, demand justice, and keep your leadership on the right path.

CHAPTER 5
FAMILY
FOUNDATION OF TRUE SUCCESS

Family is important. Do you know why? Because you came from one, and you will leave one behind.

I realize that not everyone comes from a picture-perfect fairy-tale kind of story, but what you need to realize is that when you receive the gifting of leadership, your spiritual family becomes just as important as your natural family.

As a leader, your connection to a family is one that will bring you boundless joy throughout your leadership journey. I want to expound on the three areas that I think are important when it comes to the principle of family.

- Family comes first.

- Family has the final say.

- Family lasts forever.

Family Comes First

Your family is your first ministry. I'm all for leading people and influencing the world with your content and ambitions; but at the end of the day, you come home to your family. It can be so easy to place other priorities in front of the seemingly insignificant moments that come with family—like date night and picking up your kids from school frequently. While I realize schedules get complicated and you may not have the freedom to be present with your family, you can keep them your first priority. All the projects, the companies, the meetings, the e-mails, the opportunities will come and go, but your family will be there when all the other things have faded away. If you want your family to be there for you, then you need to be there for your family. Please constantly remind yourself that your kids are growing up. They don't grow down. Time moves forward, not backward. When you make family the foundation it should be, your decisions and directions should come from a place that aligns with that foundation. When deciding, simply ask, "How will this affect my family?" You will quickly be reminded of what is important in life and what can go somewhere else.

Family has the final say

In your leadership, you will have many people tell you how they think you should lead. People love to give their two cents when they don't have to foot the bill. Although trusted voices and counsel are crucial for your leadership (as we will talk about in greater depth in Part 2), even those voices shouldn't take the place of the most important voice in your life, your family. While I do not suggest taking hiring advice from your three-year-old, I do believe the loudest and clearest voices in your leadership should be from within your family. Why are those voices the loudest? Because they should be the people closest to you. I like the way Pastor Mark Driscoll explains this by giving an example of every family getting the right to a view, a voice, and a vote. A view is a plan that comes from the parents on what is going to happen. A voice is an option for everyone to speak into that plan on what they believe would be best for the situation. The vote is even a step past the voice by letting people make their preference known. This could look like plans for a vacation or a new diet or a medical procedure you may be considering. After you hear and process everything, there is one more person who has the right to veto *anything*—your spouse. Your spouse knows you in a way that the rest of the world does not, and if they are going to live with the rewards or the regret of your decision, they deserve to get the final word. If you don't have a spouse, select a mentor in your life that has total access to your life, and submit your decisions to them. Make a commitment ahead of time to walk out what they have to say, whether you like it or not.

Family lasts forever

Your family will grow. People who started following your leadership will become family simply because they started leading with you. Some of the closest family members you have in your leadership will not share your last name. Family is a decision on the relational level, not merely determined by the biological one. Staying connected to these kinds of people is the primary reason that leaders succeed.

While visiting Atlanta before I was married or had kids of my own, I discovered that a former friend had recently moved from Texas to the city. I hadn't connected with Kevin in close to ten years, but when we crossed paths, he always had something of major value and truth to say. He's a great pastor, a great husband, and the father of four great kids. A true role model of what I wanted my own story to look like. On a long shot, I reached out to him, and we picked up right where we left off almost ten years earlier!

In a conversation about family and the natural frustrations that can come between parents, siblings, and children, he heard me out and then dropped the greatest truth bomb on me. He said, "You know Andrew, sons become fathers too."

I had never thought of it that way, and yet it was so true. Ultimately, the ones who look to you for your leadership will one day have others who look to them. It is like watching the Lion King through the eyes of Simba your entire life, and then out of nowhere, *BAM*, you have kids, and now you watch it through the eyes of Mufasa! (Cue epic uncontrollable tears!)

In the book of Genesis, Noah was ridiculed for building an ark to escape the flood; but what he was really doing was building an incubator that would carry a new covenant into future generations so his family would last forever. There would be no Father Abraham with many sons of the faith had Noah not done his part in the grand scheme of this legacy story! The principle of the family should remind you often that what you are leading will bless people in your family you will never meet. Leaders leave a legacy through the people they love in a family. Many leaders feel called to preach; I just want to make sure they are called to father and mother as well. Leaders want to do something great for God. Just make sure you're growing someone up in the things of God while you're at it. Your connection to a family cannot be broken. It must be protected. It must be treated as sacred.

When my wife Amanda and I first started dating, she said, "So tell me about your family."

I said, "I have two younger siblings who are both smarter than me, and I have four cousins on my mom's side and zero cousins on my dad's side."

Her jaw almost physically dropped, and she responded in perplexity with, "Four? You have four cousins?" Her question made me nervous (as if I wasn't allowed to have so few cousins). She went on to say, "I have like forty cousins…on my dad's side and another forty on my mom's side!"

I had a sense at that moment that my family was fixing to get larger!

Amanda's grandfather, Reverend Jose De Leon, was an evangelist and powerful man of God. While I never had the pleasure to meet him personally, I have met his legacy through his amazing family. He spent most of his adult life planting churches throughout California, Nebraska, and Mexico. He would travel from the big cities to the smallest of ranches to preach with power about the Gospel of Jesus Christ. He was always ready to encourage a pastor, play a song on his guitar, and from what I'm told, he always made you feel like you were the only person in his presence and the most special person in the world. He was a true leader, and that legacy was passed on to his children and their sons and daughters.

One of his sons, David De Leon, is one of the kindest and most generous people you will ever come across. He honors the house of God because his father honored the house of God, and that was ingrained into him. David and his wife Martha ingrained it into their four children. One who just happens to be my beautiful wife, Amanda.

Amanda has a gift for people and leadership like I've never seen before. Her presence alone is potent and everyone she meets encounters an unwavering love that melts you into a million pieces. That didn't just happen. It was ingrained into her even as far back as her great grandmother, grandma Elisa. If you do not know what to do for your family and its legacy, start with prayer. Prayer has no expiration date, and you can pray things into existence today that will manifest 1,000 generations from now.

The gifting of leadership will bring you to a crossroads in your life when you are faced with a question few leaders have the guts to answer: will you forgo personal destiny to inherit a generational legacy? Family is forever, and the gift of leadership should remind you of that every time you bring a new member into the family. Family is a principle in leadership that will keep you grounded, be supportive when others aren't, and benefit from your great leadership. Let your family lead through your leadership, and you will never lead alone.

CHAPTER 6
COMPASSION
CARING ABOUT PEOPLE

Compassion is the compass that points us towards people. Great leaders will always care for people and will be moved by the needs of people. Jesus shows us this principle in action better than anyone.

> Then Jesus went about all the cities and villages, teaching in their synagogues, preaching the gospel of the kingdom, and healing every sickness and every disease among the people. But when He saw the multitudes, He was moved with compassion for them because they were weary and scattered, like sheep having no shepherd. Then He said to His disciples, "The harvest truly is plentiful, but the laborers are few. Therefore, pray to the Lord of the harvest to send out laborers into His harvest."
> Matthew 9:35-38 NKJV

"But when He saw the multitudes, He was moved with

compassion." When Jesus saw the multitudes, He actually saw humanity. Humanity is such a huge word with an ever-larger meaning. As of now, there are an estimated 7.9 billion people on the planet.[4]

You will know compassion when you feel it. Your kid's high school game leaves you looking at the crowds as much as your son. When you see the latest earthquake in another country, your heart hurts. Jesus said they were weary and scattered, like having no shepherd. Leadership will lead you toward people that you may have never crossed paths with before. The multitudes should move you; and if they do not, let that be a red flag to your leadership. Your heart is hardening, and your passion for people is dying. In leadership, you're either growing or dying.

In 2018, Amanda and I vacationed in New York City with another couple. Once in Manhattan, we made our way to Times Square, where crowds covered every inch of the concrete jungle. You could barely walk at a normal pace, because you didn't want to run into the people swiftly passing you by. When you're in that moment, you can see every kind of person from every background, faith, and context: it's a sea of people.

When we got to our hotel room, Amanda and I had a conversation about how much compassion we have for people running their "busy lives." On a single block, a businessman boasts of his expensive suits while he gets into his privately driven car; while three feet away, a homeless man begs for bread. The multitudes should move you with compassion.

Leadership will connect you to humanity. Although it feels impossible, something deep down inside of you says, "I want to help these people."

You can't see a commercial to feed the hungry without it

pricking your heart a bit, or the hurricane of humanity on the border without it affecting you in some way. You do not have to agree with the politics for it to change your heart. Humanity is the heart of God, and that means it should be the heart of our leadership. Whether it is big or small, the connection to humanity will drive something deep within you to do what you can at that moment.

HUMANITY IS THE HEART OF GOD, AND THAT MEANS IT SHOULD BE THE HEART OF OUR LEADERSHIP.

Jesus said, "the harvest is truly plentiful, but the laborers are few." Andrew's unofficial translation: "Humanity is truly crying out for help, but the leaders are few." I realize that not everyone is called to start a non-profit and go make a difference in the world where it matters. There are some incredible organizations that simply want to help people. However, your leadership should connect you to humanity in a deeper way that causes you to reflect on the mere fact that people need guidance, help, and support. They need you to care enough about them to invest your leadership in making a difference in the best way you can.

CHAPTER 7
HONOR
HONOR IN 3D

Honor is the anchor in our leadership assignment. People tend to get confused about the difference between honor and respect, and while they are different, you can't have one without the other to achieve it properly. When we honor someone, we esteem them for the role they play; and with that comes an admiration, or respect, for who they are or what they've accomplished. Sometimes to honor someone's leadership means we show honor to the position even when we do not favor the person. On this leadership path, you find many opportunities to exercise honoring someone for their authentic leadership accomplishments; and other times, it will be a stretch to find anything beyond that their role is deserving of the honor.

Honor done correctly is a habit you should find and grow in your own journey of leadership. Where I think we miss it sometimes is we forget to honor in multiple directions. It is easy to focus on the boss or the people higher up in the organization. However, honoring those around us can be easily overlooked. I believe true leadership will require you to *honor in 3D. You are honoring in every direction of your leadership and your life.* Honor those above you. Honor those below you. Honor those beside you. Honor those who have gone on before you and who paved the road for you to walk on today. Honor those who are coming behind you.

Jesus modeled to us a type of servant leadership that flipped the cultural definition of leadership upside down. Unfortunately, there are plenty of people who would still subscribe to the thought that the "leader" is the top alpha dog whom everyone should serve and support. You may have people who subscribe to that style of leadership, but it won't come with a side of respect. I promise you: leadership is about people. When you honor from your heart, you will find yourself caring for and empathizing with people. Honoring in 3D simply means that whoever is in front of you at the time, you show and share the honor with them no matter their rank or position.

I'm reminded of a time when a group of employees was in the hallway outside my office, unaware that I could hear their exchange with one of the leaders in our summer camp ministry. Granted, this leader had been with our organization from the early days, and although he's good as gold, he has been known for his moments of "extreme"—being a bit rough around the edges. (So, I guess that would make him like rough gold, like that out of the Alaskan river in its purest form, not the jewelry case of the golden watch store.)

In a joking manner, he sent a light-hearted jab toward the group of guys with a simple, "What are y'all doing? Working hard or hardly working?" I heard it and knew that fireworks were being ignited within those guys, so I sat back and waited for the show to begin.

As expected, to the second, like a train conductor's pocket watch, each of them exploded in their own defenses and jabbed back at him. Statements like, "Oh yea, we do all the work while you sit around and do nothing all day!" and "You'd never make it a day working with us. It requires doing something!" The jabs were getting more pointed. It was time to emerge from the cover of my office.

I turned the corner with a big, "Stop it!" Jolted by the fact that I'd heard the exchange or that they had never seen that amount of emotion coming from me, I continued with my semi-mentally rehearsed speech:

> Was he wrong for saying that? Yes! But that's not for you to police. He will get handled in his own way with his own leadership; but for us, we honor in 3D, and that man that you just mocked to misery has done more for you than you may realize. The building you are standing in and cleaning daily, he built with his own two hands. Not to mention the other 70 buildings on this campus. How many have you built? He paved the way for there to even be a campus for us to upkeep and manage, and if there wasn't a campus to manage, then I guess that means you or I wouldn't have a place to come to work every day and watch campers experience the power of God in a real way. Everyone has a place to sleep, and he built those buildings. That huge dining hall where you eat every day? He built that, too. That cool figure-eight go-kart track and six-story dual water slide enjoyed by thousands each summer…guess who built those too? I'm not excusing his poor choice of wording or behavior, but I absolutely refuse to

let leaders that I work with throw shade and shame on a man whose position deserves honor. We will ALWAYS honor in 3D!

Their shocked faces quickly turned into faces of shame, and I finished with them. "You're not in trouble; you're in training. Honor will always help you lead in love first."

King David understood this well even before he was king. He honored God. He honored his father. He honored King Saul, even when Saul tried to kill him multiple times. Now, I do not think David was accepting the friend request when Saul's avatar showed up, but he understood the office and honor that a king held, and he was committed to honoring it. Honoring is not always easy on our leadership path, but it is worth it. Next time someone holds the door for you, or you pass them working in a hallway, show some honor. Remember that they are doing something so you do not have to, and they are just as important to the mission as your leadership is to the vision.

CHAPTER 8
ADMINISTRATION
PLAN ON PURPOSE

I do not know what field or industry you think of first when you hear the word "administration," but whatever pops in your mind, leadership is probably the driving force that makes a home for the requirement of administration. The origin of the word administration reaches back hundreds of years and comes from the Latin words *ad* and *ministrate*. It means service, assistance, or government. If we want to go even farther than that, we can see that in the Bible. Many times, administration or structure was used to do one thing: set order. Over the years, in many different places, you can see abuse of administration; but in its purest form, it is here to help.

Administration is responsible for things like making decisions, communicating those decisions, and documenting what has been accomplished by keeping lines of communication open. It structures authority by providing the appropriate information required to move a vision forward.

Think about a simple business contract for a second. The contract between two people outlines the expectations of both parties, the time frame within which it will take place, and what happens if either party doesn't complete their part of the agreement. Businesses see administration through their articles of incorporation and accounting procedures. In technology, it is through networking services and database management. In mass communications, you see a structure supporting internal memos as well as public messaging, marketing, and branding. Throughout your team, structure must be found within your culture, the way you care for people, and how they are entrusted to your leadership. Administration is the accountability to the gifting of your leadership.

> **ADMINISTRATION IS THE ACCOUNTABILITY TO THE GIFTING OF YOUR LEADERSHIP.**

To plan on purpose means we are structuring our decision-making not only on what we prefer, but on what is best for those we are leading. The word "purpose" implies intention. If there's a purpose, that means it comes with a side of thought and is topped with belief and faith that it is a good direction.

Leadership requires a form of administration at every level of your leading because it affects so many people. During one season of my leadership, I recognized that we needed an elaborate system of administration in order to live up to the excellence we sought in our daily operations. I knew that we needed something that could support a wide range of constantly changing information but was simple enough to use with a team of rotating volunteers. It was like trying to solve a Rubik's cube for the very first time. Just when you get one side complete, it messes up the other five. We needed answers, and I didn't know where to find them.

After searching out software companies and methodologies used by some of the greatest companies out there, including Disney, ESPN Sports Camps, and the Boy and Girl Scouts of America, none seemed to come close to what I knew could be obtainable. Because I believe that prayer works, I went for a drive and began to simply pray for an answer. In a soft whisper to my spirit, I believe I heard the Lord say, "Custom callings require custom solutions. Start building."

After a ten-year journey, a framework and software were created that we call "Phoebe." Phoebe works in all kinds of environments like churches, schools, camps, and conferences, thriving in places that gather people. Phoebe simplifies your daily operations by pairing our approach to internal infrastructure with intelligent software, keeping all information in one location. In the Bible, Phoebe was known as a "helper in the church." The Apostle Paul commended her as a trusted leader as she helped deliver his letter to the Romans. That's what this 21st-century version of Phoebe does. We help people administrate and advocate the way they work. Phoebe helps administer all your daily operations.

When you accept the leadership invitation, you also accept the responsibility to keep order, exceed expectations, and maintain structure for those around you. Jesus never completed one miracle in the Bible without two things: order and instructions. When He transformed the water into wine, He gave instructions to the disciples exactly how to prepare the jars of water. As He fed the multitudes He sat people down in small groups on the ground and gave the instructions of what to do with the fish and loaves, given by a you boy. If we accept the gift of leadership from a God who delights in order and structure, don't you think our leadership should uphold it as well?

CHAPTER 9
EXCELLENCE
AN EXPRESSION OF EXPECTATIONS

The wonderful thing about that potentially scary word "excellence" is that you are the one who defines what excellence is. I try to keep excellence extremely simple. Excellence is doing the best you can with what you have for the task at hand.

When leadership comes knocking on your door, I promise you it is bringing its best friend excellence to the party. You can't have true leadership without excellence. Excellence takes your perspective higher by requiring more of you than you are used to giving. It elevates your expectations of what's truly possible when you trust the process of leadership. When you're introduced to excellence with your leadership, you have two items that only the leader can accomplish.

1. Define what excellence means to your team.

2. Create expectations and explain them with clarity.

If your office or auditorium needs to be kept a certain way, explain those expectations. How should the chairs be set up? How do we keep them consistent from section to section? Over the years, we developed systems where we use a yardstick to ensure the aisles between each row are consistent, and a large piece of string connected to the first and last chairs in the row. Once connected, we arrange all the other chairs to line up, like using ruled paper when you write. Overkill? Not to us; it is excellence. You get to decide what excellence means to you, teach others, then hold them accountable for that excellence.

The trouble I see most people have when trying to execute excellence is the ability to keep things consistent when working with multiple teams and different people. What's the answer? A specific set of instructions that everyone follows for the same outcome every time. In the business world, we may call this a standard operating procedure or, better yet, a checklist. Whatever you call it, it is really just a *map to excellence.*

Leadership requires us to explain how we define excellence to the people who are helping us achieve it. If they do not get it right, that just proves that we didn't explain it right. I've found that the way people learn naturally plays an important role in whether that information is going to be retained or not. Some people like to read the instructions word for word and grasp information by making their own notes on what's in writing. Other people are visual learners and have to see it played out step by step. This is why people like explainer videos so much. You might think that it is dumbing down your leadership or that it is beneath you and your position. Quite the contrary, my friend. If you can't explain your excellence, you will never see it implemented by your team members.

The amazing thing about excellence is it isn't always found

solely in leaders. It is in professionals, too. I like to think of a professional as an individual who consistently creates, produces, and displays excellence in every area. I used to teach college students who wanted to step into professional media but knew absolutely nothing about it; but before they learned how to operate a camera and create amazing graphics, they had to first become a professional. With wide eyes of confusion, I continued to explain that the moment you become a professional is the moment you decide to be one.

Sure, Hollywood may have their way of doing things, and someone who's received awards for their work in the field might have their two cents about a topic; but we are just as professional as they are, as long as we consistently create, produce, and display excellence in every area. We are professionals not by our craft only but by the excellence we pair with it. Exit with excellence, knowing you did the best you could with what you had.

I think of Travis, a guy with fiery faith and a passion for people. When I met Travis as a student at our Bible school, we met while making music; since we both played guitar, we were able to connect quickly. Graduation came around, and he was interested in applying for a job with our organization. He wanted to work for me. The one issue with that was that I was responsible for media at the time, and Travis did not do media. However, I'll always hire passion over professionalism any day. I hired Travis to be a graphic designer. He had never touched graphic design a day in his life. I taught him the basics and gave him some YouTube links and solid expectations. With his creativity at its peak, Travis began to create some incredible design pieces. He was producing excellence—the best he could, with what he had. Time would go on, and he picked up video editing and increased his knowledge of camera and gear. I was so impressed with what he had become I gave him some team members to lead, and he just kept growing and growing.

Travis and I have worked together for over ten years now. His skillsets far surpass mine, and he has a true craft of excellence that will go with him wherever he goes. I'm so incredibly proud of the wisdom and excellence that comes from Travis. He has become a great leader of excellence.

> **IF EXCELLENCE IS ALL YOU PRODUCE, IT IS ALL YOU'LL EVER BE KNOWN FOR.**

If you do not have excellence in or around you, start where you are. Over time your standard of excellence will rise to new heights. If excellence is all you produce, it is all you'll ever be known for.

As with any toolbox, you pull out what you need when you need it. Your leadership is no different. Over time you'll draw on these tools to define yourself as a leader and the people around you. By keeping these tools close by, they will help you build or repair everything your leadership comes up against.

CHAPTER 10
THE INVITATION
ACCEPTING THE ASSIGNMENT OF LEADERSHIP

While you were growing up, maybe you knew leadership as the person in charge or a group of people who called all the shots. I'd like to challenge that perspective.

Leadership is not a position or a person. Leadership is an invitation to invest yourself in the development of someone else. Leadership isn't easy, and it's not always fun. It comes with its own responsibilities, and you're not always the popular one. However, when you give your leadership away for the benefit of building someone else, you, in return, are built too. Leadership is a bi-directional movement. There's an equal exchange of value between the one in leadership and the one being led. We are here for each other to achieve a mission, grow one another, and move in the direction of a future vision. The gift of leadership stands true to the fact that when you give, you actually gain.

Leadership is a gifting that empowers ordinary people to make an extraordinary difference in their world. The core of its meaning is much more than a fancy title or some flag we wave to remind people who the boss is. Quite the opposite! Leadership is the glue that carries the mission and connects it to the person willing to give of themselves. It's an endowment of power, a true anointing, gifting, that comes upon a person for a specific task and a specific time.

> **LEADERSHIP IS AN INVITATION TO INVEST YOURSELF IN THE DEVELOPMENT OF SOMEONE ELSE.**

When John the Baptist was baptizing Jesus, I believe it was in that moment that Jesus received his mantle for leadership. Was He always capable? Sure. Was He always going to be a leader? Absolutely! Yet, there is something that happens when the anointing for an assignment is accepted by a person. You can't open a gift unless you accept it first. Jesus received this leadership mantle when the Father said, "This is My beloved Son, in whom I am well pleased.", let's get real! If the clouds opened up, a booming James Earl Jones-like voice came raging into your ears, saying, "You da man!" as a perfect white dove floated down from the heavens and landed on your shoulder, I think anyone could get pretty excited about the idea of leadership at that point! Everyone wants to feel like they have that extra edge. It's that feeling you get when you walk out of a superhero movie and feel like you would rather just fly home instead of getting in the car, simply because it's easier and you CAN! Or is it just me?

I was in a meeting one time with a team member asking him if he would be willing to take a promotion in leadership for the ministry. He had been with the organization for a while and was very consistent in his work. His day-to-day duties were pretty routine, and I could tell there was more inside of him. This promotion was going to require him to oversee a team of about ten people, manage schedules, and interact with a lot of older people who had more experience. As I sat with him that day and asked him if he was ready to take on a greater role in his leadership, he reluctantly looked at me and slowly said, "Do you think I can do it?"

My response without hesitation was, "I know you can do it!"

It's completely normal (and smart) to want to feel confident before you accept a role that will require sacrifice and responsibility.

This is the special secret sauce that takes the average and makes them anointed. All through scriptures and history, we see average men and women accept the invitation of leadership and achieve remarkable things.

- Moses led the Israelites out of Egypt.
- Nehemiah became Bob, the Builder.
- Rehab changed the lineage of her family tree.
- Elijah conquered witchcraft.
- Daniel stood up to a dictator.
- Esther voiced injustice.
- David took on the fight for a nation.
- Paul upheld the Gospel.
- Jesus secured eternity.

Is that a natural ability? It's the driving force behind the gifting of leadership: it promotes people and transforms them into great leaders *after* they accept the invitation. Every one of these examples contains the same simple equation. Individual + Invitation to Leadership = Transformational Change

What could you do if you accepted the invitation? How much could you affect the course of history, industry, or your family tree? What lives would be different if you stepped up to the plate? The gifting of leadership assures you that when you step up, you don't step up alone but with an anointing for the job ahead.

A few years back, I took on the role of managing a seasonal staff for the summer camp program our family has led for over thirty years. Based on the number of responsibilities we had to cover, we knew there was a certain percentage of students in a graduating class that we had to have in order to meet our numbers. Up until this point, if you wanted to join the team, you waited until applications opened, went in for your interview, and then waited for the length of the dreaded *Jeopardy* theme song to get your answer on whether you made the team or not. Over a ten-year period, the interest level had declined so much that we weren't hitting the numbers needed to run the operation effectively. I knew it was going to be tough to convince a bunch of twenty-somethings to give up their summer to serve at a summer camp. Can you see the poster now? "Give up your summer for long hours, multiple dorm mates, and screaming campers for eight weeks!" Yep, the line was pretty short for applicants. Instead of the application process, I transformed the application into an invitation. Two weeks before the actual hiring process began, I sent out a specific letter of invitation to a large group of graduating students. In the letter, I explained that the leaders around them had observed leadership qualities within them that could be developed if they had a place to do so. Discovery Camp could be that place. We offered some extra incentives that probably motivated the select few, but it sparked something in the students, and before you knew it, we had a 93% acceptance percentage from our invitation, and applications doubled because there was a crew of people already on board and ready to make ministry happen. Everyone loves being invited. Though it may not have been theologically sound, the film *Angels in the Outfield* painted a great picture of what happens when someone is there to give you an extra hand to get where you're going. That's what we were doing: giving students a chance to step into a new world and build their gifting of leadership.

Leadership is not a respecter of person, gender, or social status.

Anyone can connect with the deep inner drive of leading.

All you have to do is accept the invitation.

Leadership isn't climbing a ladder for success; it's landscaping to see what you can plant in the lives of others and watch grow. Too many people are trying to turn leadership into a destination to be the keynote speaker at some trendy conference that won't be around in a decade. I want to see leaders who will invest that same energy and passion into building the people entrusted to them, multiplying their influence, and guiding them as they grow. That's real leadership. Real leadership plants seeds, pulls weeds, and protects the fruit. Fake leaders fake their fruit, ignore the weeds, and steal the seeds from other people's trees. I'm not against influence; but I would rather influence the influencers because then it's not solely about what my leadership accomplished. It's about what our leadership accomplished *together*. Leadership is the glue that holds the vision together. All it needs is someone brave enough to look past themselves and accept the invitation of leadership. That someone can be you.

Part Two
The Leader | The Giver

You can be a leader. Even without formal training or extensive academic experience, if you can make a choice to be a leader, you can be a leader. As John Maxwell notes, "Leadership is influence."[5] It is impossible to have leadership without having a leader. There are many phenomenal definitions of what it means to be a leader. Mine is simple: *A leader is a giver—someone who gives. Someone who serves.*

Anyone who is willing to serve others and give of themselves in the many ways required of leadership is one worthy of the true title of "leader." Jesus said that He came to serve, not to be served. (Matthew 20:28) In Romans 1, Paul describes himself as a "servant of Christ Jesus." The reputation of what it means to be a leader drastically changes from one decade to the next; but one thing remains true: a leader is someone who changes and influences the circumstances of a specific space. You do not have to have a title at your job or thousands of followers online to become a leader. You become a leader when you make a choice to invest a piece of your life into the development of someone else.

There's a classic children's book written & illustrated by Shel Silverstein called *The Giving Tree.* At first submission to a publisher, it was rejected because it seemed too sad to be a children's book and "too simple" for adults. When a different publisher, Harper & Row, decided to take a chance on it, they published the first run of a little over 5,000 copies in 1964.

The simple story follows the relationship between a boy and

a tree. When the boy is in his younger years, he wants to climb all over the tree and eat the fruit of its branches, and the tree gives. As he gets older, his requests of the tree change with the nature of his needs—wood for a house and limbs for a boat. The tree continues to give. The story concludes with the tree being whittled down to a stump, and yet he still has something to give the boy, who is now old and unable to stand. The tree gives him a place to sit down. Although it is a book for children, there's so much we as leaders can take away from this fictional story.

Leaders should be givers—constant givers. The book that has now been in print for fifty-seven years still is used to show the power of giving to audiences of every age and all over the world. To date, the book has sold more than 8.5 million copies and has been included as one of Scholastic's "100 Greatest Books for Kids."[6]

When you have made the decision to give of yourself, you will begin to feel the true fulfillment of what leadership provides to every person who chooses its adventurous path. Let's look at a few things that define what a true leader is and does.

- A leader is responsible.
- A leader is solution-minded.
- A leader is always present, yet always in the future.
- A leader recognizes and honors their place of authority.
- A leader makes it aware that there is always somewhere else to go and other people to help.
- A leader helps make the impossible possible with practical paths of how to get there.

- A leader isn't moved by circumstances but rather creates a current for navigating them.
- A leader lives today as he wants to be remembered tomorrow.
- A leader can see the invisible and help others see it, too.
- A leader sees opportunities instead of problems.
- A leader loves, believes in, and holds people accountable.

When you choose to be a leader, you are placed right in the middle of purpose, and that gives you something to strive towards every day. Where do you find this purpose? The purpose is found in one of two areas: your greatest passions or your deepest pain. When you find your purpose, you will find the area that needs a vision, and where you have a vision, you need a leader.

Everyone can become a leader if they are willing to change the way they think and act. You can't be a leader if you're selfish, and you won't be an effective leader if you simply in it for personal gain.

Leadership requires leaders who understand that in the end, it is not about *what* they build but rather *who they build*. You can build anyone, anywhere, anytime—it is the most fun and fulfilling part of leading.

So, if your interest is piqued and your heart is beating a bit faster, keep reading! Let's start learning more about the expectations and experiences we will walk through when we decide to be a leader.

CHAPTER 11
THE JOURNEY
MOMENTS AND MILESTONES THAT MAKE US

Enjoy the journey, and never grow tired of the view.

People are very familiar with this vocabulary and visual imagery of what a "journey" means. It is all around us. We see it in our movies, hear it in our songs, and experience it through life events like births, graduations, weddings, and even funerals. Here's the big reveal and the most significant moment of this book so far. Are you ready? When you accept the invitation to leadership, you're saying "Yes" to a journey. This journey will not only take you from point A to point B. It will pull stuff out of you and place stuff in you throughout the entire process. In the fast-paced world we live in, it can be difficult to slow down and recognize that your leadership is a work in progress, and it is going to take time to appreciate the fullness of life that it brings to you.

Over the years, I can look back on this short stretch of leadership and see the moments and milestones that have been a part of my journey thus far. Your journey is full of places, people, and even purposes for a specific season that are all a part of making your leadership what it is today. The rebellious team member who completely destroyed the culture you were passionately building is just as important as the mentor who gave you an hour every month. Both make up the journey! When you start out on this journey, you typically are attempting to change, fix, or build something; and by the end of it, you realize it actually changed, fixed, and built you. I try to constantly remind young leaders: as you build the vision, the vision is building you. In the great words of the deep and well-esteemed scholar Olaf, from the Disney movie *Frozen* says, "We set out to change the forest, but I think the forest actually changed us." Well said, fictitious frozen dude!

AS YOU BUILD THE VISION, THE VISION IS BUILDING YOU.

The journey comes with all kinds of unknown adventures, but the areas I want you to really focus on are *moments* and *milestones*. The significance of a special and even spiritual moment in the journey of your leadership is something that money can't buy, and fame won't allow. These moments do not have to be long; but when they happen, you know it and you feel it! You realize that something just shifted in your heart and in the spirit, like Peter Parker getting bit by a radioactive spider. Before the moment, you're a high school kid, and minutes later, you're scaling walls with your hands and feet and flying through the city, one web sling at a time—moments matter.

MOMENTS

I had the honor of enjoying some life-impacting moments with Evangelist Reinhard Bonnke at our world leadership conference in October of 2017. He has since passed away physically, but his spirit and impact on me and the entire globe live on.

Born in Germany in 1940, Reinhard knew by the age of nine that he was called to do something great for God. His father was the pastor of a small church, but pastoring wouldn't be the only thing his life would be called to. Later in his adult life, he and his wife Anni felt the call of God to bring salvation and the power of God to the country of Africa. His largest single crusade took place in Lagos, Nigeria, with over 1.6 million people in attendance.

After decades of meetings and crusades all over the world, we were honored to be one of his last public speaking engagements in the United States. I knew that his time with us would be a moment for my journey. We've had the honor of hosting many special and significant ministers in our lifetime.

Brother Kenneth Copeland dedicated our sanctuary in Columbus in 2004, and Dr. T.L. Osborn dedicated our church in the Houston/Katy area a year later. When you've experienced many of these significant moments, you learn to forecast them as they come along your journey. I knew the importance and significance a few moments with Evangelist Reinhard would bring.

My brother Peter and I hosted him with honor for a little

under twenty-four hours, but his mark on us will last a lifetime. In the car ride from the airport to the hotel—something I have done hundreds of times with other guests and leaders over the years—he spoke with us in a way that was conversational, yet challenging and commissioning all at the same time. While much of the conversation was very personal and private to my own life journey, let me share one of his comments with you today.

Evangelist Bonnke had so much faith in the impossible. He believed in things that most people wouldn't even think to imagine. He shared a story about how his team wanted to print 7 million flyers for a crusade they were hosting.

His response was, "NO! Print 8 million! I'd rather have one million too many than not have enough for people who need to meet Jesus!"

An extra million fliers? That makes my operational brain twitch just a little bit, yet it makes my faith ignite for what is possible when we believe God for something huge! It is a good thing he printed those fliers because over his lifetime; he would personally see over 79 million people come to Christ! His passion for Jesus and commitment to the power of the Holy Spirit place his life and legacy as a general in the faith.

Why would a man with this much anointing and influence take the time to build up two young guys in ministry? Because he's a leader.

When you have moments like this along your journey, you recognize that it is the calling upon your leadership that guides you to the spaces and conversations that you need to develop yourself for the journey. There will be moments that surprise you, challenge you, or convict you; but each one is important to your leadership journey.

Milestones

What is a milestone? We've already touched on this briefly in chapter two, but let's expound on it a bit more right now. It is goals, positions, markers, trackers, whatever you want to call them; they are the pins in your map of mission that says, "I'm doing the right thing and going the right way." These are the opportunities that present themselves to you and are truly gifts in disguise.

In the earlier years of my leadership, I would get consumed by comparison with others. It was crippling. I couldn't go to an event, concert, or watch anything on television or YouTube® without pointing out all the things that they were doing well and all the things that I was not doing. When you are consumed with someone else's journey, you are guaranteed to mess up and miss out on your own. That is why social media can be a huge distractor to our time and focus. (More on that in future chapters.)

To not get distracted or destroy my own journey, I wrote down three lines that I looked at almost daily for a long time. "Head down. Heart open. Keep moving forward." The last part was inspired by *Meet the Robinsons*, the greatest and most overlooked Pixar film of all time—the movie my firstborn toddler refers to as "The Dinosaur Movie." I'm not really sure why, since there's only one dinosaur in a very short scene; nonetheless, I know what he means.

Now in a much healthier place, I have learned how to celebrate what others are doing and evaluate what I'm doing to see what can be implemented into my assignments and projects. You wouldn't travel non-stop in a car on a road trip without stopping for fuel, would you? Milestones give us the ability to take a pause from the trip and see where we are to confirm where we are going. Jesus used miracles as milestones on his journeys. If he wasn't performing miracles, he was either teaching or traveling. When miraculous things begin to take place in your life, you can take that as a hint from heaven that you're moving in the right direction. How do we see these miracles in the journey? You will see them large and small. It may be the open door that became available at a job that you weren't expecting or extra attention from an avenue you weren't expecting.

I'm reminded of all the milestones we've seen during our summer Discovery Camp program. About seventy miles west of Houston, in the country town of Columbus, you will find 1,088 acres where over half a million campers have *discovered the difference* that Jesus can make. Since 1989, we've had multiple milestones that have defined and shaped Discovery Camp and made it what it is known for today. Here's a brief recap of the milestones we've seen throughout the years. The very first summer, instead of 500 campers, we saw 5,000 with zero marketing. By the mid-90s, church groups were traveling from more than thirty states to bring youth and kids' groups. One youth pastor that I always have admired would bring his students from Indiana has said, "I pass 1,400 camps every year to get to Discovery Camp because I know the power of God will be there." Those kinds of comments are milestones! They confirm the calling on your leadership.

One night the camp kitchen caught fire, and the staff woke up to an opportunity to get creative and feed 600 hungry campers. When the state said we'd have to shut down for the summer, we repaired things and got things operational again within six days so the remaining camps could take place. That was a milestone of grit and determination. It defined who we were as a staff.

Right around the turn of our 30th season of Discovery Camp, I got a call from a friend who was working for CBN at the time. He informed me that he and his producer were going to be in Texas for a few days, and they wanted to do a story on the camp and all the crowds and miracles we'd seen over our thirty years. We accepted the invitation, and the night it aired we were inundated with calls and website traffic. This was a milestone of celebration for the camp. It didn't change what we were doing. It didn't stop the train so we could restructure how we do camp. No, it simply was a nod, a wink, a pat on the back that said, "You're doing great! Keep going!"

I think the spot did more for us as a staff than it did for those who watched it. It was the milestone we needed in our 30th year to set our sights on the future and go for more! You can see the spot at TheGiftOfLeadership.com/dc.[7] Milestones will meet you on your journey when you least expect it and when you need them the most. It reminds you to pick your head up and remember that this is a spiritual thing. It is bigger than what happened in the last e-mail you just archived. It places purpose back into what you are doing, and it refuels your leadership for more greatness ahead.

The journey is about the flow of faith. It doesn't happen overnight. It takes a lifetime, and sometimes it will even require someone else's lifetime to teach you something about yours. When I hear the stories of faith from the men and women of God who trusted that "If God said it, that settles it," it builds resilience in me to withstand whatever may come my way.

The journey won't come without jolting, but it always provides what you need and who you need to see your leadership strengthened. Wherever your leadership journey takes you, do not forget to enjoy it. Enjoy the laughs. Enjoy the problem-solving. Enjoy the ability to develop gifts in you and others. Enjoy the progress, and do not focus on perfection. Never grow tired of the view. What's the view? The view is the positive effects your leadership is bringing to the world. Leadership is not about a destination; it is about the journey—enjoy it.

CHAPTER 12
THE PROMISE
DREAMING & LEADING INTO THE POSSIBLE

*For all the promises of God in Him are Yes, and in Him Amen,
to the glory of God through us. Now He who establishes us with you
in Christ and has anointed us is God, who also has sealed us
and given us the Spirit in our hearts as a guarantee.*
2 Corinthians 1:20-22

I have this crazy obsession with peanut butter and jelly. As a kid raised at a gigantic summer camp in Texas for church groups, I always found myself bypassing the hamburger and hot dog lines and asking for peanut butter and jelly. Fast forward thirty years, and I still annoy my wife by responding to her "What do you want for lunch?" with "I'm good with peanut butter and jelly." I know I am not alone in this love obsession with this godly creation! Some things just go better together. Batman needs Robin. Salt and pepper. Hot Cheetos and cheese. (I actually can't stand this snack; but my wife loves it, and this book is dedicated to her. Shout out to the 956!)

Whether it is a sandwich, superhero, or spicy treat, there are certain things that are just meant for each other. So is the case with the promises of God.

Do you know there are over 7,438 promises in your Bible directly for you? Our Father God loves making promises to us and what's even better is that He never forgets His word! If He says it. He will do it! Even though the promise is only a single word, it actually comes in two parts. 2 Corinthians 1:20-22 tells us that all of the promises of God are *YES* and *AMEN*, or another way to say it would be "Yes and SO BE IT!" It is God's way of giving us a "Yes," as any good Father would, and then also agreeing with us. It is almost like He is saying, "Yes, that's a really good idea!" When He agrees with us, it is a stamp of approval throughout all time and beyond. The promises of God are *YES* and *AMEN*.

Promises are powerful. They can be an anchor in troubling times and hope for the hopeless. They can fuel your faith in the impossible and bring comfort when we lack understanding. To have a promise from your best friend is one thing, but to gain one from God—the creator of creation—puts it on a different level. When you receive the promise of God, you are attaching faith to what you already know to be true.

Leadership is that undeniable force that is privileged to escort these promises from an eternal space to an earthly place. How so? The promises of God are so potent they have to be distilled down into two parts: dreams and visions.

In every leadership journey, you will be placed in a season and position to dream or lead (build). Dreaming is the process of downloading the heart and vision of God. Dreams acknowledge and activate the promises when you accept them by faith.

Leading is the act of taking that dream and constructing it into a vision.

The power of leadership gives you the ability to reverse engineer a promise into existence. By leading a leader through the dreaming and leading of that vision, you can proclaim that the promise that came from the Father has been fulfilled.

In 1 Chronicles 17, King David receives a promise through the prophet Nathan. It was a promise that would promote and protect his family.

> And now I'm telling you this: God himself will build *you* a house! When your life is complete, and you're buried with your ancestors, then I'll raise up your child to succeed you, a child from your own body, and I'll firmly establish his rule. *He will build a house to honor me, and I will guarantee his kingdom's rule forever. I'll be a father to him, and he'll be a son to me.* I will never remove my gracious love from him as I did from the one who preceded you. I will set him over my house and my kingdom forever; his throne will always be there, rock solid.
>
> 1 Chronicles 17:10-14(MSG)

Obviously, David is excited about this word and does what every single leader does when they get excited about a dream. They blast off and try to make it happen in their own strength. (Never a good idea!)

Nathan quickly corrects and corrals David by saying something along the lines of, "Whoa, whoa, whoa... No, you can't build the house; your son Solomon is going to!" Confused by this statement, David tries to better understand the meaning of the prophet's words. Nathan helped David understand that because of his war victories, there was too much blood on his hands. The instructions were that someone who was pure of these deeds would build it, and that leads us to Solomon.

> And David said to Solomon: "My son, as for me, it was in my mind to build a house to the name of the Lord my God; but the word of the Lord came to me, saying, 'You have shed much blood and have made great wars; you shall not build a house for My name, because you have shed much blood on the earth in My sight. Behold, a son shall be born to you, who shall be a man of rest; and I will give him rest from all his enemies all around. His name shall be Solomon, for I will give peace and quietness to Israel in his days. He shall build a house for My name, and he shall be My son, and I *will be* his Father, and I will establish the throne of his kingdom over Israel forever.'"
> 1 Chronicles 22:7-10

When God created you, he gave you this incredible ability to imagine things: to see the unseen. Go to a place in your mind and heart where what doesn't exist actually exists. It is the power of seeing the impossible become possible. If you want to lead, you have to be able to dream!

Now this is a very different kind of dreaming than what you do when you sleep. This kind of dreaming is the lifeblood of leaders. It is what fuels your passion for more. It is what gives you the drive to keep pressing into things when vision gets hard or stuck. Leading yourself in your dreams gives you the upper hand when life may be giving you a thumbs down. I believe every leader needs a daily dose of dreaming.

In high school, I wasn't the strongest student on paper, and I continually found myself floundering on my way to a passing grade in multiple classes. As Amanda and I like to joke, "Hey, we made it! C's get degrees!" (I'm not saying that education isn't important for every academically inclined person I just offended. I'm digressing.) The point is, while I was in school, most of the time, it was dreaming that got me through the day. Dreaming gives you permission to build worlds that do not exist yet, and your leadership is what develops that world into a reality. Take a daily dose of dreaming: it'll make your life as a leader more enjoyable and remind you what leading is all about. Dreams are visions without a strategy. You receive dreams, but you **build visions**. David's dream became Solomon's vision.

The dreams in our heart are often a reflection of what we are our called to do with our lives. When someone is dreaming, they are tapping into the promise that is assigned to their life if they accept it by faith. Taking the step from dreams to realities is what converts the *what if* of a dream into the *what's next* of a vision. Most of the time, people will find their dream in something that marries what they are passionate about and what causes them frustration. Let's say you love animals but hate seeing them homeless on the side of the road, so you decide to create a local animal shelter because your town doesn't offer one. Boom!

Vision is the ability to see the unseen and the never-been-done-before, then find the strength and strategy to see it built from the ground up.

Vision is the part of the promise that has a plan. When you have a vision, you have a promise with purpose, and that vision becomes your assignment. You must care for it, nurture it, and protect it because it is being entrusted to your leadership.

We must have assignments because that's how we build the kingdom.

For the past twenty years, I have engaged with the leadership calling to support the ministry my parents founded. Understanding that it was my father, Tommy Burchfield's role to dream, and my job is to lead, I started catching on to a funny pattern in our conversations. In a chipper and excited mood, he'd say, "Hey, I'm just dreaming but wouldn't it be great to…" I began to realize that this phrase meant my to-do list was fixing to grow. Why? One dreams, one builds.

If you know Tommy Burchfield, you know that he's a visionary to the max and a builder in his own right! In his early days of ministry, he hosted a Christian Day at Astroworld and gathered 7,000 people. That's vision!

After a successful season of ministry in Houston, my parents followed the call of faith to a cow pasture outside of Houston to build up the summer camp for independent church groups you heard about in the last chapter. Now, thirty-five years later, over half-million kids and churches from all over the world have experienced the power of the Holy Spirit in a real way. Discovery Camp is a special place. This man is not a novice when it comes to building vision, cultures, and places! He went on to build a bible school that has alumni in 39 states and 42 nations around the world, and he's currently building a thriving world church in the region. Oh! Did I mention he did all this debt-free too?

You can imagine the shoes I felt had to be filled when my time and season of leadership approached. However, every leader has a reason for a specific season. It was by the providence of God that I would be gifted and talented to integrate technology, teams, and systematic administration that would allow for the infrastructure for their dream to be built. One dreams. One builds. "Old men will dream dreams, and young men will see visions" (Joel 2:28).

I believe that's what the prophet Joel saw. He saw the promises of God coming into existence between generations. My prayer is that the younger generation of leaders will have the patience to see the wisdom the older generation has to offer. The same goes for the older generation: that they would recognize the gifting and talents in the younger leaders who can truly *see* how to accomplish the vision they have for their future.

Scripture shows us many examples of these "dream team duos" who would dream and lead great things. These were the people in the Bible who had a vision for something and attached their faith to a dream, and were ready to build something. Moses and Joshua delivered the Israelites from slavery into the promised land. Elijah and Elisha kept the position of the prophet potent in a day when doubt and unbelief filled the land. Paul and Timothy established the Gospel of Jesus Christ by planting and pastoring churches. God the Father and Jesus Christ the Son rescued mankind from the eternal mistake of sin and reconciled humanity back to the original design of proximity to the Father.

Principles of the Bible will always transcend whether a person subscribes to the faith or not. They are true and can't be changed. Even in the corporate world, we see examples of this dream and lead principle. Many would argue that Steve Jobs dreamed up Apple and Steve Wozniak built it in the early days. Larry Page and Sergey Brin invented Google. William Procter and James Gamble gave us Procter & Gamble. Henry Wells and William G. Fargo developed the banking system we know as Wells Fargo. John D. Rockefeller and Henry Flagler started Standard Oil and revolutionized the industry. Warren Buffett and Charlie Munger dominated the real estate game with Berkshire Hathaway. Bill Bowerman and Phil Knight made us all feel like we were all Olympian athletes simply by putting on something that has a Nike swoosh on it. Mike Krieger and Kevin Systrom created a little photo-sharing app that was eventually sold to Facebook for $1 billion dollars. (You've probably heard of it…it's called Instagram.) Brothers Walt and Roy Disney decided to create the *happiest place on earth*, and now Disney is a household name around the globe.

Now I know what you're saying to yourself: "Andrew, that's great; but I'm a one-man band. It sure would be nice to have someone around me with a skill set to really build my dream." Let me be clear when I say this: anyone can dream and lead at the same time. To fully understand the process of a promise, you must know how to do both: dream and lead. The problem I see is people don't understand that what they are trying to do requires the two separate parts we've discussed: (1) a dream that is never built stays a wish, and (2) a vision that doesn't have anywhere to go becomes a stagnant deteriorating thought.

Leadership will always keep you involved in dreaming and leading, reviving the dream, building the vision, and confirming the yes and amen of Heaven. Do not despise your dreams. Do not think that because it has never been done, it shouldn't be done. The people around you are there to support the dream and vision God has given you. Find your place. Find your people. Get connected with someone who has a dream so large it is scary. Wayne Meyers, a missionary to Mexico for over seventy years, once said, "If your dream doesn't scare you, you're not dreaming big enough."

Solomon ended up completing the temple on behalf of his father David well after King David had passed. I've heard it said this way: sometimes it is not about what happens in your lifetime, but rather in your lifeline. David knew that his dream transcended his life. He knew Solomon would have to pick up the baton of promise and keep running.

Why does the Apostle Paul instruct us to "run with endurance" the "race set before you?" (Hebrews 12:1) He doesn't say the whole race, just the part that is before you. Whether you are dreaming or leading the vision, know that it all started with a promise; and if He says it is going to happen, it is going to happen. It is not always easy, but it is always worth it.

Recognizing and accepting the role you play in the vision will bring fulfillment instead of frustration. If you are suppose to be in the driver's seat of vision as the key leader taking people to another destination in their life then you should dream. Dream on! If you're assigned to help someone build out that dream, then lead! Lead and focus on building what is in their heart to see. By playing your part, running the race set before you, without worry or anxiety about the part of the race others are running, you will limit your frustration, be more productive, and ultimately you are sowing seed into the ground of your own future. Leadership will give your life a promise worth dreaming into existence and a vision that changes circumstances around you. Accept it. Develop it. Build it. Leave it for others to benefit from it.

CHAPTER 13
LEADING YOURSELF
SECRETS & SYSTEMS TO STREAMLINE LIFE

When I started in leadership, I was so overly confident that as long as I showed up to the meeting on time, ready to give directives, cast vision, and all the fun fluffy leadership stuff, then I would be able to walk into the house at the end of the day, hang up my imaginary leadership cape and avoid the responsibility of leading myself.

How wrong and dangerous that was! The truth is that leading yourself is the ultimate priority in everyone's leadership journey. If you can't lead yourself, then you do not deserve to lead others. I like the way Craig Groeschel puts it: "Leading yourself is a direct reflection of how you will lead others."[8]

The pressure of leading yourself will quickly evaporate when you discover the following:

- Leading yourself doesn't mean you're perfect.
- Leading yourself doesn't mean you get it right every time.

- Leading yourself doesn't mean you are committed to a way of life for the rest of your life.

When you make the decision to lead yourself, you open up a new avenue into your heart and mind that gives you permission to essentially practice on yourself. From time to time I will find myself giving myself a mental pep talk to get through a task or a commitment that I have procrastinated on. That's leading! It is giving yourself permission to identify the difficulty of something while simultaneously pushing yourself for the progress you desire to see. For decades, leaders have been leading themselves into places and spaces that have been uncomfortable.

Self-Awareness

Self-awareness is the tool of choice for the mature leader. If you are going to be honest with yourself about the areas you need to grow and lead in, this is how you accomplish it. A telescope helps you see what's far off. A microscope helps you see what's deep inside. By constantly seeing the big picture and zooming in on granular details, you will learn things about yourself that you can apply to your daily leadership and life. Let's apply this lens to reverse-engineer some unconventional ideas surrounding self-awareness in your leadership.

There are three areas that help you in leading yourself.

- Discipline
- Delegation
- Disconnection

Discipline

Every leader needs a form of discipline if they truly want to be effective in your leadership. The beautiful thing about discipline is it can be found in every area of your life: spirit, soul, body. I think Jesus knew that discipline was so important that He gave us the daily cue of what it means to be a *disciple* of Him.

Discipline will look different for different leaders. For some, they love waking up at 5:00 a.m. and disciplining themselves on a 5-mile run; for others, that sounds like cruel and unusual punishment. Maybe you need the discipline to exercise and eat right, or perhaps you need the discipline to not check your e-mail on the weekends. What about staying disciplined to actually finish a project you've started! Discipline to show your spouse how important they are to you. Effective leadership requires daily self-discipline; it's not an option or suggestion if you choose the path of leadership. It is a requirement that rewards in ways that very few will live to see.

Delegation

It might not seem that a word like delegation would appear in a chapter about leading yourself. Although delegation involves a second person or system, it is nonetheless important when leading yourself. Your role as a leader is to lead. Profound right? Sometimes leaders get stuck in the rut of taking back responsibilities that they have already let go of. If we do not delegate, we are actually holding someone else's gifting hostage. Unable to grow. Unable to be a part of building a great vision. When we delegate, we are leading ourselves by not allowing our ego to get back into the spotlight with an "I can do this all by myself" or "Well, they just do not know how I want it, I'll do it better." (If they do not know how you'd like it, that still falls back on your ability to communicate vision, not their ability to execute the vision.)

Delegating gives people the ability to own a piece of the vision. If you only delegate responsibility but not authority, too, then you're just micromanaging. No one likes a micromanager! When you delegate, for your own leadership health, give the whole thing. For all the control freaks out there, here's how you cope with your loss of control. Start by delegating something that, if missed or messed up, wouldn't cause too much of a catastrophe. Every leader has to earn the ability to lead. If you can't trust them to deliver information at a specific time, then how will they be able to uphold an entire department? After a few wins of consistently delivering what you've delegated, level up a bit more with more trust and more responsibility. I assure you, the people who care about their leadership will never disappoint. Delegate something today. It helps others but, in return, reminds you to lead yourself and focus on what only you can do.

Disconnection

I think leaders can become disconnected when they get too familiar. It is the same thing over and over: there's no challenge…no real focus; they think they are on cruise control, but they are really just idling. Familiarity will always end in the fatality of your leadership. You've seen the coaches on the side of the sports games that are really into what's going on in the game. They are energetic, yell at players, and disagree with referees. They are active! Then there are coaches who simply sit on the sidelines, fold their arms and let everyone else do the coaching. They got familiar with the game, and in return, the players lost respect and started taking orders from someone else. Do not get familiar. It causes an immediate disconnection from your leadership. Stay connected to yourself, your soul, and your spirit.

Another area that can cause leaders to become disconnected is their pride. They can't admit when they are wrong. They always have to be right. It is rarely about what "we" are doing and always about what "I" am doing. Pride is a problem in leadership. When left undealt with, it is like a poisonous plant that continues to grow and will ultimately overgrow your leadership. It is one thing to take pride in your work and to be proud of it, and it is another to find your identity in it. Pride will disconnect you from your vision, and your connection to leadership and all the responsibilities that come with it will suffer.

FAMILIARITY WILL ALWAYS END IN THE FATALITY OF YOUR LEADERSHIP.

Stubbornness causes disconnection when leaders are unwilling to change. Change is the one thing you can always count on in life. I've always had a hard time understanding why leaders are so resistant to change. They should be the ones initiating it! If a leader has a problem with change, they also have a problem with vision. Change should affect every area of the leader's life consistently.

Do not fall into the dysfunction of disconnection. There are too many people who are counting on your leadership.

The Value of a Life System

When you lead yourself, you must be able to manage every part of…guess who? You! This includes everything from your emotions to your time and energy. I remember the season of life when I really began to take my productivity seriously and tried to bring order to my life. At first, it seemed like a chore or something I was being forced to do; but in reality, it was because I was leading myself into a better way of doing my life. Leadership will spotlight things inside of you that cause you to question, "What would it be like if…?"

Do not toss those questions out too fast! Those questions—answered authentically—may be the key to unlocking a brand-new way of living for yourself as a leader. By taking account of your life and your leadership on a frequent basis, you can change things that aren't working for you and those around you.

I'm a big believer that every leader needs a life system. What is a life system? It is a way to help you do exactly what we are talking about: lead yourself. Think about it. We have systems for our finances called banks. For our health, hospitals; and for the way we learn, schools. Rarely though, do we have people teach us about managing our time, accomplishing effective work, and having enough energy to be truly present with the people we are with to give them the greatest impact we can as a leader. I won't tell you how to create your own life system because I realize that it sounds incredibly intimidating to many people out there. However, imagine a life where you could recall any piece of information that you've encountered that made an impact on your life or the ability to have everything you need when you sit down to work.

There are plenty of great coaches out there on the internet who can teach you how to maximize your productivity. One of them is a candid Canadian named Mike Vardy. I had followed Mike for many years and learned so much from him via his podcast and blogs. One night he had tweeted that he was going to be in Austin, Texas, which is about ninety minutes from where I was living at the time. On a whim, I reached out to this influential written blogger and productivity ninja, to see if I could treat him to dinner. To my shock and surprise, he agreed.

We had a great time geeking out over productivity, and he gave me some insider secrets and tips I could use to tweak my life system a bit. As the conversation grew to a close, we briefly discussed the importance of having one's life in order and how that was truly the ultimate honor to those around us. I left that conversation inspired and impressed by Mike and his willingness to sit down with me and speak into my world, with very little knowledge of who I was. Although we come from two different places in life and spiritual belief, we both deeply agree on this: when you lead yourself, you are actually doing it to benefit those around you. It is a gift to your family, your team, and your friends to have your own life in order.

When things are in order inside of you, it gives you time to focus on the things that really matter on the outside, too. In 2017 when Houston and much of the South were hammered by hurricane Harvey, of all the people that reached out to check on me and our organization, Mike was at the top of the list. I'll always appreciate that random night with that Canadian blogger who put purpose to my productivity. If you're just getting started in building a life system, start with the top three areas of your calendar, a project manager, and a note-taking app.

> YOU WILL NEVER EFFECTIVELY LEAD ANYONE ELSE UNTIL YOU CAN AUTHENTICALLY LEAD YOURSELF.

See something that inspires you? Take a picture a put it in a place where you can see it again without scrolling through your entire photo library to find it. Have an idea for a blog post? Write it down and process it later at a time and place where you can really bring it to life. Having each of these tools gives you what you need to create greatness—a calendar to manage your time. A project manager to prioritize what's important to you, not what everyone else thinks should be important to you. A way to reference notes that you created or curated on areas that add value to life. Having a life system will help you organize and structure your life in a way that won't make you feel like everything is constantly spinning. This happens for every leader at some point, and when it does, recognize that you've got what I call "vision vertigo."

Being self-aware is not something you do once a year or at the quarterly staff meeting. I believe it is our responsibility as leaders to be self-aware in all that we do. You will never effectively lead anyone else until you can authentically lead yourself. I like the way Peter, my brother, says it when he is coaching people about preparing their leadership for the future: "Lead yourself and stay focused on your future."[9]

In the end, you are responsible for yourself. They are your choices, your thoughts, your work ethic, your attitude, your actions, your future, and your legacy. Leading yourself is a never-ending process and changes frequently, but if you can be truly self-aware, you'll be in a place where you can know yourself, love yourself, and, most importantly, lead yourself into great places.

CHAPTER 14
VISION VERTIGO
BALANCE, BOUNDARIES, AND BUDDIES

Do you remember that game when you were a child called "dizzy bat"? Maybe you have a different name for it, but I promise you this: you've played dizzy bat! It is simple: you grab a baseball bat (or stick if you were raised in the country like me), and you bend over, placing your forehead on top of the bat. Now with whatever motor skills you have available, you begin to spin in circles around the bat, keeping your head firmly planted on the end of the bat. After about ten times or so, you quickly stand up and begin to "walk straight." Most of the time, it is a good laugh for everyone who WASN'T on the bat because the person is stumbling all over the place just trying to walk a straight line. After ten rounds of the dizzy bat, no one is walking straight.

Sometimes life and leading can feel the same way. You are going around and around being faithful, consistent, and everything in between. Then when you stand up quickly, you realize that you do not recognize the vision you are leading or the life you are living. I call this "vision vertigo."

Now I understand that vertigo is a real medical condition, and I'm trying to minimize its effect on an individual's quality of life; but vertigo serves as an effective allegory for losing our sense if or grasp on what is really in front of us at the time. Vision vertigo can take place in your work, in relationships, or your personal life. Every person goes through some exceedingly difficult seasons in life at some point, and sometimes you may feel that your life is so upside down that you are not fit to lead anything or anyone. I have hope for you today. You are not alone. You may be grounded right now, but you will fly again. To combat these radical feelings of being unstable and out of control, you need these three things:

- Balance on the inside.
- Boundaries on the outside.
- Buddies all around.

It's not easy, but it is worth it. Let's understand more about what vision vertigo is. The symptoms of vertigo include swaying, tilting, or having a sense of unbalance. To me, vision vertigo is that feeling or sense that you've lost your footing in the vision. Things that used to feel solid have gone soft. Areas of certainty have morphed into questions. If you are not careful, you will spend so much time in this tailspin that after a while, it will not only affect the vision, but it will affect you. Medical professionals say that vertigo is caused by a dysfunction of the inner ear.[10] I do not believe that is too far off for the leader, do you? When your inner ear (or your spirit for this analogy) begins to feel off, you can tell that something just "doesn't feel right." It is like you are being pulled in a direction that you do not want to go in.

Vision vertigo takes place when you don't feel like you are hearing what the Spirit is saying about your position or footing in the vision. I think it is safe to say that no one likes this feeling. No one gets on a boat for a cruise and says, "I can't wait to feel like the floor is falling apart!" Remember, our gifting of leadership comes with an understanding that the vision we are upholding belongs to Him. We are simply the onsite foreman, ensuring the job is completed to His criteria. That can be difficult to do if you feel like you aren't getting the instructions you need.

Leaders love stability. What do you do, though, when you do not feel that stability? What do you do when you feel like things aren't in balance? What do you do when you're too exhausted to make things right, or the team or financial position just isn't in the right place? I will tell you what to do: when the vision feels unbalanced, counterbalance it with your self-leadership. If you feel like things are not in the right spot, then chances are *you're* not in the right spot.

Whenever I feel the vision isn't going in the right direction and I have vision vertigo, I tend to start by blaming it on others or circumstances. What the solution really is, though, is me getting in touch with myself and my spirit man and tightening things up.

BALANCE ON THE INSIDE

We are made in the image of God, meaning we have a spirit (eternal), a soul (will and emotion), and a body (flesh or earthly vehicle). If those areas are unbalanced, our lives and our efforts to lead vision will be, too. You are the leader. You are setting a course. You are charting the path. If you're unbalanced, how can you not expect the vision to be unbalanced as well? The nice thing about this self-reflection is that it is so easy to adjust and get things back on track. Let's bring balance to the parts inside us that make us who we are to start with.

SPIRIT **- S**PIRIT **F**IRST**, S**YSTEM **S**ECOND

Every person has a spirit. The Bible is clear about that (see Romans 8:16). When we accept Jesus Christ, we gain access to His Holy Spirit. The Holy Spirit is all-knowing and is described in Scripture in many ways, but some of the examples use words like teacher, helper, and comforter: all words that aid believers in their day-to-day commitments. You do not have to lead alone. You can lead with the power of the Holy Spirit, day in and day out, on every single decision you make. Christians affirm that the Holy Spirit knows everything, and the Holy Spirit is always right. Making decisions can be difficult. Allowing the Holy Spirit to help you is the wisest thing you could ever do as a leader. One thing the Holy Spirit will remind you of in times of vision vertigo is your commitment to the kingdom assignment. Without going too deep here, we know that we have been assigned as a leader by our Heavenly Father to achieve a specific mission on this earth for His kingdom and His glory. Impact and influence are not only possible, but expected in your assignment!

When I play with my kids, who are toddlers right now, I will sometimes hold them in my arms and then gently lower my arms quickly and raise them back up again. It creates a brief sense and feeling that they are falling. They begin to laugh, and we do it another ten times. Why would I make a silly movement like that? Because it forces them to hold onto me tighter, and I love their hugs. There's a natural tendency to holding on tighter to things that feel like they are uncertain.

Do you do that, too? Think of the logic of that for a second: this is falling apart, so let me grab ahold harder to the thing that's falling apart. When things feel like they are falling apart in nature, you have to double down on what's not carving in, your spirit man. Be reminded of your assignment. Take authority over what you have been given authority over. Spend some time in prayer, silencing the distractions around you. In the natural, it might not seem like grabbing ahold of something falling apart is wise. However, we lead spirit first.

See, my kids know that regardless of what it feels like, they can hold on to Daddy. You can hold onto the Holy Spirit. You can trust Him. You can lean in so intently that you will know exactly what to do.

The greatest leaders are the ones who remain the greatest followers. A life lived that follows the Spirit is an exciting life! It brings an energy that your natural man will never be able to create on his own.

I have a value that I uphold daily. Spirit first; system second. Faith is a spiritual thing. Belief is a spiritual thing. Listening to the leading of the Holy Spirit or the voice of God is a spiritual thing.

Facts and feelings are systematic. I believe they are all part of balancing yourself on the inside, but I will always side with spirit first, system second. Make prayer your first response, not your last resort. When your spirit man is balanced, everything else will quickly align, and the spinning will begin to slow.

Soul | Free to Feel

The hardest conversations are the ones you have with yourself. Your soul is a large part of those conversations. Every single year people spend countless amounts of money on "soul care" because they realize the value that a great inner dialogue can have on every part of your life.

When your emotions are spinning around from vision vertigo, you will notice that things you used to get excited about do not excite you anymore. The people who seek out your leadership are a bother rather than a blessing. These are the warning signs to pay attention to. How do you care for your soul? Mental balance is so important. Maybe you need to turn off the movies and TV for a while. Perhaps you need a break from those social media streams? When we are around anything that causes competition or comparison, we are guaranteed to find something that will eat away at our soul.

How do we fight against that soul drain? Find a routine and system that keeps you on the mission. Consistency is the key for you in this season, my friend! This is not the time to experiment with new friends and unfamiliar places. When the vision is spinning and feels unbalanced, you want something strong enough to keep you grounded while you re-calibrate your soul to the mission and purposes of your life. I like to say, "Do not forget to bathe as you build."

Find something you enjoy and do it often! Maybe it is going for a walk or playing a game of chess with the family. It does not matter what it is; if you enjoy it, that's all you need to do. Give your soul a chance to find space again and watch how a recently dull life begins to find its color again.

Body | Healthy is Happy

I used to despise the word health because my perspective and mental picture of health was the fit and healthy athlete on the cover of GQ that was upholding unrealistic standards for how "men" should be. While I think it is great to be physically fit and be in a physical place where you can enjoy life and the movements it brings, I do not want you to confuse health with fitness. It is health AND fitness for a reason. Being healthy means being whole—having true awareness of how your body is feeling and functioning. (Emotions play a big part in this too).

When I turned thirty years old, I knew that health was going to have to make its way to the center of conversation in my life, and I was terrified. I didn't have any rhythms or rituals that kept me healthy. I was too focused on vision, work, progress, ambition, status, and million more items completely out of order in life. It seemed like every leader I heard, read, or talked to were all saying the same thing: *"Focus on your health!" "Take care of your health!"*

In my naïveté, I figured they were just talking about physical health, getting to a gym, and eating my fruits and veggies more often. Since I knew I wanted a true lifestyle change, I decided to become a student of the topic for five years. I tried to consume content on everything health-related to find where I wanted to plant my flag of discovery and get on board with whatever that tribe was pushing. Not knowing where to begin, I decided to just follow what became my golden triangle: movement, nutrition, and rest.

I'm not saying I have it all figured out, but here's what I do know. How you rest impacts how you make decisions; and that is fueled by the movements you make with your body, which will be determined by the food you eat. Leading yourself can feel complicated, especially if you do not understand everything about a particular topic. You know what, though? Every "expert" had to start somewhere, too. Make your best step towards better and watch improvement happen all on its own. When you get in a better place, and the vision doesn't feel like it is spinning so fast, then you can dive deep and develop your leadership by developing yourself.

BOUNDARIES ON THE OUTSIDE

Dr. Henry Cloud and Dr. John Townsend, who authored the *New York Times*-bestseller *Boundaries*, define a boundary as "where I end, and someone else begins, leading me to a sense of ownership. Knowing what I am to own and take responsibility for gives me freedom."[11]

It's amazing to me how a word that sounds so limiting, like "boundary," is actually all about freedom. When life is spinning from vision vertigo, freedom sounds nice. Place some boundaries on the things you can control, and it will offset what you cannot. What are some practical examples of boundaries on the outside? Going to sleep at a consistent time every night is a great start. Avoid engaging in gossip around the office. If you work from home, turn off "work mode" before your kids get home from school so you can be fully present, not cooking dinner while dictating an e-mail to your phone. Boundaries are put in place to help us, not hurt us. Can you imagine if there were no lines on the highway to signify where the lanes were? What if we took the traffic lights out of the equation while we were at it too? No boundaries on the roads at all…what do you say? That would be a disaster waiting to happen. If you are not familiar with Dr. Henry Cloud, I encourage you to check out his phenomenal contributions to leaders and people in relation to their mental and emotional health. His courses, found at boundaries.me,[12] have been instrumental in my life; and because I know his life and counsel are biblically-based, I know I can trust him. He is one of my virtual "buddies" and one of the few voices I listen to almost every single day. Why? Because we show up to our leadership with our emotions and ourselves every single day. Boundaries will help you slow the spin down long enough for you to find your footing again.

BUDDIES ALL-AROUND

A "buddy" is a good friend. Good friends are ideally situated to help mentor us. While the idea to have a mentor is a very trendy thing right now, it dates back to the days of the Bible. The Apostle Paul was a mentor to Timothy and many others all throughout the New Testament. It is always a good idea to have a mentor or someone in your life that can shoot straight with you and tell you what you need to hear, not always what you want to hear. A buddy can also be someone who knows the real you and is willing to just be with you as you go through a difficult time in your life and leadership. They can be friends, family, or someone with the same occupation as you or has lived a similar experience. The wonderful thing about technology is we can stay connected to anyone anywhere in the world to help us become stronger.

I am grateful for the people in my life that talked sense into me when my world seemed like it was suffering from vision vertigo. The challenges we face in life become the lessons we teach others while leading. I had a therapist[13] tell me (I believe in Christian counseling) at the end of every session for over a year, "Andrew, don't forget…there is a God, and you're not Him."

I will find different buddies to watch and learn from based on the areas in which they've been successful. One guy might have a successful business, but his wife cannot stand him. That is not the guy I want marriage tips from. Do you know what I mean? To have buddies all around you means that while you are spinning with vision vertigo, have enough people around you to support the areas of your life that need the most encouragement at that time.

Mentors do not have to be exactly like you, and these days you can have virtual mentors that guide you through the content they produce and provide to the world. Anyone who speaks wise counsel into your life and has the fruit and experience to show for it is worth listening to. Do yourself and your leadership a favor, learn from the people who have already figured it out, and do not make mistakes that could be avoided. A good mentor is like a good mirror. They show us the areas in our lives that, if not taken care of, will affect us and those we are leading.

Vision vertigo won't last forever. It can't last forever because people are counting on you to lead them! Having balance on the inside, boundaries on the outside, and buddies all around will keep you in a safe space while you navigate the difficult waters that come with life. Learning how to be self-aware is a skill. It's worth mastering because you will need it to know what kind of leader you genuinely want to be.

CHAPTER 15
TYPES & TYPOS
CRAFTING AND CREATING YOUR PERSONAL LEADERSHIP IDENTITY

One of the most exciting and intimidating portions of your leadership in development is deciding what kind of leader you want to be! It is like junior high and high school when everyone is trying new clothes, new hairstyles, and hanging around different people trying to find their true friends. It can be a little overwhelming to pinpoint your purpose and develop your leadership personality.

Over the years, I've come across hundreds of leaders who struggle with this. I've seen people up close and personal, and I've observed from a distance. We have to remember a few things before we pick apart different leadership styles. Number one, leaders are people, too. They have emotions and bad days just as you do. They are sometimes placed on a pedestal, usually for one of two reasons: either they were placed there involuntarily (and normally will do their part to get off it as quickly as they can), or they are insecure and need constant affirmation and affection to uphold their own personal identity. These leaders tend to put on an invisible superhero cape and rush into people's lives and management duties to save the day.

I have noticed some key traits that can help identify potential pitfalls in a person's life and leadership. I've packed these points together with themed profiles that will help us spot some of the leaders that are out there. I'm sure as you read through these profiles, you will be reminded of someone you know. You may even see yourself. I am not saying that every leader fits into one of these categories: these are just examples of what can happen when our leadership style reflects only certain attributes of our lives.

THERMOSTAT LEADER

My brother, Peter, and I were invited to be a part of an exclusive behind-the-scenes look at a large school district many years ago. It was a nine-month program that met on the first Thursday morning of each month. It was inspiring.

This school district is known as one of the best in the state and is sometimes compared to the size of a small city. They have their own police force, for crying out loud! I learned a valuable lesson from one of the senior executives. Prior to being hired, he told the board, "Now, if you want a massive change of course and to take things in a different direction, I'm not your guy. I'm a thermostat leader. You set the temperature, and I'll adjust the culture to go where you want it to go." I thought that was great phraseology.

Thermostat leaders keep everything in order and do not

rock the boat. Stability is important to the thermostat leader. The thermostat leader is the one who can see when things are getting a bit too hot or a bit too cold and can adjust the culture accordingly. What do I mean by too hot and too cold? Too hot means people are edgy; there's a lot of stress, maybe from intense schedules, unresolved frustrations, or a lack of vision. Too cold means people are simply passive to the mission and vision. They do not have that initial spark they used to. Thermostat leaders are great at doing their one thing, and they do it well. However, when it is time for massive change, you'll need to change your leader.

Thunderstorm Leader

The one predictable item in the world is how unpredictable weather can be. True? It can be sunshine and blue skies in the morning and a big Texas-sized thunderstorm after lunch. A thunderstorm typically starts off in the distance, and you can see it coming. At our house, we can see sheets of rain coming down the road. So, with fair warning, we can prepare and get inside quickly. The storm is fierce and comes with its fair share of loud crashing booms of thunder and unexpected, shocking blasts of lighting; and yet just as fast as it starts, it also blows through and ends. Some leaders are like this, too. You just know when they are walking down the hallway, they are fixing to unleash on you. They open your office door or meet you in a certain spot and unleash wrath and fury upon your life. It might be all the things you did wrong for that given day, week, or month, or it could be a massive list of things to do by the end of the day. They talk fast. They talk a lot. Their points of communication are all over the place, and it is hard to follow what they really would like from you. Like lightning and thunder, you are simply riding out the storm of this conversation.

If you have been around a leader like this before, chances are you know that sometimes just riding it out knowing that the storm will pass quickly is the best advice you can give yourself. A thunderstorm leader comes, drops everything they have in one sitting, and moves on, unaware of the potential damage they just caused. If you are a thunderstorm leader, try to listen to the people around you so you can recognize what you are doing and some ways you can lead better.

Trophy Leaders

As a millennial, let me confess I think the whole "give a trophy to both teams" thing really backfired on us. I played soccer when I was in grade school. One year I was on a team called the Dolphins; we scored zero points the entire season. Not a joke, ZERO points! So the next year I changed teams. I was a fierce competitor in the second grade, and I wanted to be on a winning team; so I got "traded" to the Sea Hawks. We only scored ONE point the entire season. Although we only scored one point in two years of soccer, in both years, we still got a championship trophy. I get that it was participation and all that, but what it did to every little undeserving millennial kid out there was make them think they were entitled to a trophy, even when they did not deserve it.

Some leaders play the same game. They want to flaunt their success in the world without having worked for anything. They boast of large social media audiences but fail to mention they purchased fake followers. They care more about their own ego than they do about building the team. Anytime the team does something amazing, they take all the credit by alluding to the fact that they were the ones with the grand idea and the intelligence to pull it off.

Trophy leaders are not fun to be around. They talk about themselves constantly and because of their own insecurities, believing in people is extremely hard for them to do. When another leader talks about something they are proud of or a goal they just accomplished, the trophy leader reaches over the conversation, grabs the spotlight, and viciously pulls it over to shine bright on themselves. Their attempt to gain advantage typically taints the conversation, and leaves people feeling drained and unmotivated. A trophy leader is always lifting their trophy higher than the rest and bragging about their accomplishments, instead of celebrating others. The trophy leader should not be confused with those who are simply proud of what they have accomplished. It is absolutely okay to talk about and share our genuine achievements with the world; but if we are being disingenuous or failing to celebrate others and their contributions to our successes, we must examine our motives and re-calibrate how we interact with others.

Toxic Leaders

It is sad that this category has to be included in those we call "leaders," but it is true. Even in leadership, you will find a few bad apples every so often. How do these people even attain their status? Loyalty, family relationship, or sometimes they are really strong in one specific area of their job, but the other 90% of them is just awful.

What's a toxic leader? Toxic leaders are the ones whose

actions bring more harm and dysfunction to the culture than good. Every good leader should always be growing the best parts of their team and culture, but toxic leaders are typically so consumed with themselves they do not have time to care about anyone else. You will see this played out through narcissistic traits, poor motives, and extreme insecurity.

I was once assigned to a temporary team that had a leader who was known for doing some shady and crazy things but had never experienced it for myself. After only about two months, I could tell this person was not here for the right reasons. Insane demands that did not take the rest of the team into consideration at all, unrealistic deadlines so they could look like they were ahead of the pack, and zero empathy when someone came to them with a concern or a problem. One time a guy on the team finished up his assignment a bit earlier and was going to jump in and help someone else on the team finish theirs too, and they were scolded and belittled because they "couldn't follow the instructions." I remember taking these frustrations to a mentor of mine and just talking so bad about this so-called "leader," their response to me was simple and yet profound.

They replied to me with, "Well, Andrew. At least when you're a leader, you'll know what NOT to do."

I still think of that moment often.

Toxic leaders damage the morale of a team and the confidence of an individual. They thrive on taking credit for things they did not do and desire to always be the smartest person in the room and never give anyone a chance to develop their own leadership skills.

This is not what it means to be a leader! If you are in a situation where you have a leader who is toxic, try to see them as first a person and then as a leader. Not the other way around! When you try to see their leadership first and then are let down by their actions, it can be hard to connect with them as a person. It is possible to not like their leadership and still follow their lead. It is biblical too. We can show mercy to the person and still honor the position.

David was not a huge fan of his boss, King Saul. I mean, seriously, how would you like it if your boss envied your success, tried to murder you, and wanted all the popularity you were getting. Yet, David realized the importance of honoring the office of the king. The position that Saul held at the time was one that deserved honor, despite the toxicity he brought into it.

Look at your leader through the eyes of compassion, and it will change the way you see them as a person and give you the strength to follow their lead within their position. When the time is right and in the right setting, speak up about your experiences with your leadership to someone who has the authority to bring change. That may be a supervisor, a representative of Human Resources, or someone higher up in the organization.

Sometimes you might have to get the police and local authorities involved, too. Never ever should anyone claiming to be a "leader" force you to do anything that is illegal, immoral, or uncomfortable. Any person who abuses verbally, emotionally, physically, or sexually should be reported through the proper channels without hesitation or regret!

Toxic leaders are toxic because we allow them to be. Find the time, find the way, and speak up about the areas that are damaging to you and those around you.

The Tiny Truster

I could have easily just called this micromanaging, but it didn't start with a "t," and that would have thrown off the entire vibe of what I'm trying to do here! When someone leads in a "tiny way," they are really saying they do not trust anyone to do a job they've been assigned. To be fair; sometimes, that is justified. If you have no management experience or are in an organization with high turnover, having employees turn in work that is sub-par or riddled with mistakes fosters mistrust and increases the temptation to micromanage.

Tiny trusting leaders are those that need constant feedback from their team and want to know how every step of the process is going to take place. There's a big difference between giving a vision for what you want to see done and giving the road map for how you want each individual step completed. I've heard it said, "A team decides how to take the hill. A leader decides which hill to take." Giving your ideas sometimes tends to seem like a dead-end, and productivity suffers because you spend more time talking about how to accomplish things instead of accomplishing things! I must admit, from time-to-time analysis paralysis can become a real thing for me. Trusting yourself and the voices around you will help you understand how to move things forward without getting pulled into the weeds of details. In the end, you bring people onto your team to help you accomplish a mission and vision. If you are constantly doing your job and theirs too, you are missing the point and leading in a very tiny way. Start slowly and give out tasks that will be a success no matter what happens. If you have a team you can't trust, you truly do not have a team at all.

Crafting and Creating Your Identity

Leaders come in all shapes and sizes and have completely different types of personalities. Some are loud and lead with a charge of boldness and pioneering attitudes. Others are soft and steady and are happy with their typical unchanging routine of life. You will encounter all types of leaders on your journey, and it is important to take the traits you love about certain leaders and discard those you do not approve of. Eat the fish and spit out the bones!

You are in full control of the type of leader you want to be, and with constant trial and error, honest feedback from those around you, and a student-minded openness about what you can improve, you will be proud of the leader you choose to become.

Developing your leadership is a lot like typing. It starts with getting acclimated to the keyboard. Then you get comfortable and speed up, moving the keys at a faster pace and delivering the words from your head to the page. Just when you feel like you found your groove, BAM! You missed a key, and made a mistake. The dreaded typo throws off your groove and requires you to stop and evaluate what just happened. After deciding that the typo shouldn't be a part of the masterpiece, you slowly reach up to the top of your keyboard and hit "Delete." A sense of accomplishment and restoration enters your soul, and you can try again to deliver the original word of your intention.

That's developing your leadership identity! You will do some things you love, and then boom, something will happen where you say to yourself, I do not like the way that came out. That's not the kind of leader I want to be. When this happens, do not be down on yourself. Just figuratively delete that attribute from your mind and move on to develop what you do love about your leadership! Remember, typos are going to happen, but it doesn't give them permission to stay in the chapter of your leadership unless you allow them to.

Write your leadership lifestyle in a way that is easy to read and leaves a legacy to learn from.

CHAPTER 16
LEGACY STARTS TODAY
FIVE BEHAVIORS GREAT LEADERS DO DAILY

Your legacy as a leader begins today. It can be discouraging to hear about those who have been leading for twenty years when you are simply trying to survive the next twenty-minute conversation with someone. While the principles, depth, and spirituality of our leadership are vital, don't let them become an obstacle to becoming a leader who leads with simplicity, one day at a time. Regardless of what's on the agenda for the day, focus on these five areas if you want to leave a legacy with your leadership.

LOVE PEOPLE

You do not have to know them to love them. You do not even have to lead them to love them. All kinds of people are a part of life. You will cross paths with some of the most intelligent people on the planet and some of those most "interesting" ones too. I love them all. Jesus said to love your neighbor as you love yourself. That's why self-worth is so crucial. Get whole and know who you are so you can turn around and love others into who they are as well. A lack of identity will only produce a lack of authentic love. Love is the greatest commandment of all. Lead with love.

Think about the person and what is going on in their world before you blast things from your to-do list for the day. Have empathy for where they are in life. If they show up five minutes late, do not scold them; lead with love. Recognize, for example, that she's a single mom who has three kids at three different schools across town, but she still shows up to volunteer on her only day off. People need to know that they are loved. They need to know that someone in this life cares about them and the things that concern them. You can be the leader who does that for them. I used to have leaders say, "I do not know if I'm doing this leadership thing right." My response has always been, "If you're loving people, you can't do anything wrong." Our school of ministry coined a phrase that is planted deep within our students: *Jesus is our passion, and people are our priority.*

My brother-in-law and equally great leader, Ryan, has this nailed! He loves everyone, and everyone loves Ryan! When you walk into a room that Ryan's already in, the world stops so he can greet you and tell you how awesome you are. It is an instant confidence booster!

Loving people will instantly shift the focus from you and remind you what the point of your leadership is all about. Lead with love through every conversation and even every confrontation. Love people. People are the only thing that matter in this life.

BELIEVE IN PEOPLE

I was in a long line at the grocery store one time, and the guy in front of me started making small talk. After we talked about some of the immediately obvious things like the weather and sports, he asked me what I did for a living. I answered, "I believe in people." He smiled and asked how I landed such a great job. We both laughed, and then it turned on some light bulbs for me. Everyone wants someone to believe in them. I can't think of anyone greater than my friend, Gabe Muñoz. Gabe introduced me to praise and worship teams and has developed hundreds of vocalists and produced over 30 albums. His secret sauce? The phrase that would ring in your ear whenever you were around him: "You're the best at what you do." Gabe believes in people like rocks believe in gravity. It is a guarantee that you will be believed in when you get around Gabe, and that does something to your insides that lets you know it is safe to believe in yourself because someone else is believing in you already.

While it is the primary role of the family, we all know not every family unit is wired in a way to provide that kind of support. That's why we all need to do our part with the people entrusted to our leadership. Believing in people means you see past their present and into the potential of a person. It means you create a vision for them that they might not have set for themselves. When

> **BELIEVING IN PEOPLE MEANS YOU SEE PAST THEIR PRESENT AND INTO THE POTENTIAL OF A PERSON.**

you believe in someone, it is an immediate jolt of validation for their life. Will they make mistakes? Yes. Will they let you down? Yes. Will they try to quit on you? Absolutely. What do you do then? Cue up the Journey tune, and *Don't Stop Believin'*! What would have happened had Jesus stopped believing in Simon Peter? I mean, he had every right to stop. Here's a guy who has been as awesome as he has been an annoyance. He's chopping off people's ears and doing the very thing he said he wouldn't do, deny the Christ. Oh yea, and he didn't just do it once. He did it three times! If that were me, I'd be saying, "three strikes: you are out of here, buddy!" Thankfully, I am not God. Jesus kept believing and giving an opportunity to the man who would ultimately be the apostle the entire New Testament church would be built upon. You never know who is in front of you and where they will go in life. When they get there, you will be glad that all they can say about you is that you never stopped believing in them.

Forgive Fast and Move Past

We forget about forgiveness, or we just overlook it because it is so hard to do sometimes. If there is anyone who needs to forgive, though, it is leaders. It can be as simple as an administrative mistake that left you feeling embarrassed because it made your company appear unprofessional, or some deep emotional wounds that are hard to forget. The level of offense does not give the leader a right to bypass the process of forgiveness. People take advantage of and betray leaders without even breaking a sweat all the time. It is a beautiful thing to be a servant-minded leader, but it equally places you in a spot that gives people easy access to trample over what you've made available to them. When someone does you wrong, goes behind your back, or hurts your feelings, please forgive fast. Forgiveness is sometimes done as a step of faith. Forgiving someone and still processing the hurt is a positive place to be in. I'm not saying let people just run over you at their own will, but realize that in leadership, there is pain; and there will always be a need to forgive people.

There was a guy on my team years ago who did and said some things to me that were extremely hurtful. It was necessary to address some integrity issues with him; but he didn't appreciate the correction and exploded with anger and rage. He used every word in the book and spat at my face as he furiously ran for the door. Although the things he said were completely inaccurate, it didn't change the way it hurt. It hit hard. There's never a leader who wants someone to be hurt like that, regardless of what the situation is. I wish I could say I forgave him instantly, but that's not how the story goes. I held on to it for far too long, and eventually, I found it within me to forgive him for his actions. Many years went by, and one day I received a voicemail from a number I didn't recognize. At the other end of the phone, I heard his voice, shaky and almost scared, as he asked for forgiveness for what he had done and how he had left the ministry. He went on in his message to say that for the past few years, not a day had gone by that he didn't think about that moment and how he wishes he would have handled things differently. He thanked me for my leadership and said that he missed working for me. I quickly called him back, accepted the apology, and we had a wonderful conversation that repaired what was broken.

Forgive fast, leaders. If you don't forgive, you don't grow. It will begin to settle into every area of your life. It will affect your decisions, your health, how you communicate with your team, and your perspective on what it means to lead in general. It is not worth it.

IF YOU DON'T FORGIVE, YOU DON'T GROW.

Sure, I know there have been some horrific things that have happened to you. You may not be able to forget, but it doesn't give you the right to withhold forgiveness. Jesus said, "Forgive them, for they know not what they do" (Luke 23:24). When people do hurtful things, most of the time, they do not know what they are really doing. They commit horrible actions in a place of hurt, confusion, or frustration; their lack of emotional control causes them to do things they would never choose to do under normal circumstances. Forgiveness should be the strongest muscle you develop in your leadership. It is easy to believe in people; forgiving them can take some work. I like to say, forgive fast and move past. Do not remind them of the time you forgave them for that one thing ten years ago. When it is done, it is done.

Push People

I hope you just got a true visual of physically pushing people. Where that is not all encouraged or endorsed, it does make for a funny mental image. Limiting beliefs are a real thing that people face, and part of the ways that we believe in people is we push them past their comfort zones. We help them believe a different narrative about themselves, especially what they are capable of. Matthew, an insanely creative motion graphic animator, was hired to take the motion graphics of our television show up a notch, and boy did he! He far exceeded expectations. Though he was incredibly charismatic, his job never gave him the opportunity to work with anyone else. I knew that was going to hinder his leadership development. Matthew came to work every day on time and never caused an issue with anyone; but if he was going to become the leader I knew he could be, he would need an assignment that pushed him outside of his comfort zone. I remember it vividly: I walked into his office with no warning, shot into the silence and said, "Are you ready to develop your leadership?"

Surprised by my extremely dramatic entrance, he looked up from around the gigantic monitor in the middle of animating something, laughed, and said, "Uhhhh…sure." I began to tell him how I wanted to move him from the department where he worked mostly by himself to overseeing a completely different department that had nothing to do with his skill sets and overseeing about twenty people. He looked at me with wide eyes with a "What was in your coffee this morning?" kind of look.

I went on to tell him that I knew he was never going to truly develop his leadership if he were to stay in this office, animating layers of graphic files for the rest of his days. We had to shake things up if he wanted to grow, and I knew he could do it. I promised him I would stay close and help him out however I could. He thought about it for about forty-eight hours and then accepted the position. He stared the very next day. Matthew developed himself over the next few years and developed an incredible department that still uses many of his procedures to this day. The best part was that as he moved on from our organization, he stepped right into management roles that allowed him to lead people and oversee a lot of resources! Sometimes the gift of leadership means you have to push people a little bit. What happened to the media animation position? We dialed back on our animation for a while and used some templates until Devon showed up, and then we pushed him, too.

Ask for Help

Leadership isn't meant to be done alone. Even the Lone Ranger had Tonto. Do not be afraid to ask for help. It may be from someone older and wiser or younger and cooler. Asking for help is not a sign of weakness: it is a sign that you care about your mission and your leadership, and you want it to be the best it can possibly be. We've already covered the importance of having a mentor (everyone needs someone who can help develop them), but sometimes you have questions that are unrelated to you. It may be something as simple as noticing that a certain person always has their clothes looking so great and is sharp as a pin, and your clothes seem to have an invisible sign that invites every wrinkle in the region to join the party for presentation day at the office.

KNOWLEDGE IS POWER, BUT EXPERIENCE IS USEFUL.

Ask for help. Knowledge is power, but experience is useful. It is one thing to Google an answer and get the info, but seeing it in action from someone who can help take you to the next level quickly is where growth takes place. Imagine leading a project with a small group of people and it becomes overwhelming because the team is just not clicking. C'mon, we've all been there. One person is doing all the work, and the other is doing none of the work. You know it is your responsibility to produce something great, and you have a deadline staring you in the face.

Instead of suffering your way across the finish line, take a moment and learn something by going to another project leader or even your own boss and saying, "Listen, I'm really trying over here, but it doesn't seem like I'm making much progress with keeping the team balanced and unified. Have any tips?" When you ask for help, you are humbling yourself and opening your leadership up to the idea that it is time for an upgrade, like a software update that has to be installed on your phone to make things better. That's what asking for help does. It helps your leadership and gives people an invitation to lend their expertise and their perspective. I was working on some insurance matters recently…everyone's dream job, right? I came across some items I didn't understand. I didn't stress about it or research till my fingers fell off. I just picked up the phone and called our agent and asked, "Can you educate me a bit more on this, please?"

Within moments light bulbs turned on in my brain, and I was in a better place to make a decision that was going to affect the entire organization. When you have a question, ask for help. When you do not understand something, ask for help. If you are too prideful to ask for help, ask for help anyway. Your leadership is here to enhance not just the people you are giving it to, but it is here to help make you better, too. Learn from the wise, lean on your team, and always ask for help with anything.

Living Legacy

If you focus on nothing else in this book and simply follow these five behaviors throughout your daily leadership, you will finish your leadership journey with a strong legacy. Leaders exist for the sole purpose of seeing people reach their fullest potential. The items mentioned in this chapter will help your leadership in achieving that life-giving goal.

CHAPTER 17
F.A.C.T.S.
BUILDING THE TEAM

One exciting part about leadership is that you do not have to take on the mission alone. At the beginning of any leadership journey, you'll be required to find people who are willing to go with you on this mission of changing the world. John Maxwell says, "If you want to know if you're a leader, just turn around and see if anyone is following you. If not, you're simply taking a walk in the park."[14]

Followers authorize your leadership. Now before you let this get to your head because you have "followers," let's keep this in context. Followers are people who trust you to take them somewhere. They are trusting you to take their family somewhere. From Frodo Baggins to Han Solo, convincing people to join you on your journey is a tall order. Anyone willing to follow you is handing you an invisible application to be on the team. Teams are what bring the vision to life, and to understand the best use of the team, you need to know the F.A.C.T.S. about teams.

- F - Frame up the team you need
- A - Atmosphere & attitudes affect everything
- C - Communicate for your culture
- T - Training the troops
- S - Success scales

FRAME UP THE TEAM YOU NEED

Frame up the type of team you need, not the one you want. Most leaders hire people just like them, and that is not a wise idea when you are trying to grow a vision. Yes, you want people who believe in you and what you want to accomplish, but they should arrive to help with a different skill set than what you already have.

Have you ever seen builders frame up a house? They move quickly, and before you know it, a few boards become a wall, and then a few more boards become a roof. Before you know it, you have an entire house in position, all made of the same type of material. Teams have to be framed up as well. Putting the right people in the right places could determine if the team is effective or not. You can make the teams as large or as small as you need. Knowing the type of team you need should be considered as early as possible. Teams are made up of different positions. Think about it: a football team or a rock band have different members, all executing different parts of the mission but unified in their end result. A rowing team, on the other hand, must be in unison, all flowing in the same motion to achieve seamless success. When you are framing up your team, ask yourself what positions do I need to be effective? If you're in a church context, you made need people who are multi-talented and can handle many different roles on the weekend versus the rest of the week. If you run sales for a booming startup, you need people who execute a formulaic approach to their calls, documents, contracts, and notes without getting bored or losing enthusiasm. When you frame up the type of team you need, then you can assemble the right people.

Atmosphere & Attitudes Affect it All

Atmosphere and attitudes are the building blocks of a great day for your team. I like to call them "the Double A's." It's very rare that you would adjust one without affecting the other. If you're the leader, you're responsible for keeping a strong pulse on these driving forces within your team. When my shift leaders would come in and ask what the agenda was for the day, I'd smile and say, "Change the batteries!"

Because so much of a team's success is a mindset, it's important that we do our part to help that mindset stay on track with a mission. The atmosphere you create should be positive and full of light and life. Appropriate music can really help, too. When you walk into the room, you are walking into an atmosphere and attitudes. Maybe you are walking into a conversation full of deep questions, or a practical joke that just took place, and the entire room is laughing hysterically. (Those rooms are great to walk into.) When you walk in, you walk in with authority to change the atmosphere and the attitudes where needed.

In the book of Hebrews, we read that Jesus had more joy than all his companions (Hebrews 1:9). You should have that same kind of joy. People want to be around someone who loves what they are doing, not waiting to punch a clock at quitting time and run out of the room like Fred Flintstone with cartoon dust clouds following them. I would tell the team to put two AA batteries inside their pocket. When they felt those batteries, I wanted them to remember the priorities of leading: atmosphere and attitudes. Jesus never left a location the same way he found it. He always walked away leaving more life, more joy, and more purpose. Attitudes rub off on others like wet paint. You can feel when someone has a bad attitude, but no matter what it was that got them into that funk, you have the ability to get them out of it! Leaders care about people.

Our role is to refocus their attention on the reason we are doing what we are doing. That's why having a mission and vision is so important: it gives you something to point your team members to all year long. Adjusting attitudes is like a pilot adjusting altitude. You must do it gradually, and I'd suggest you always start with what's important to *them* before you talk about what is important to you. Ask about how things are at home and let them share from their heart. After you've let them go first, you can begin to adjust the altitude of the conversation by reminding them of why we are here doing what we are doing. Stories or memories from other successful moments of their journey will serve you, too, as you make the climb to better altitudes. At some point, however, they must make a choice about where they are going to land. Will the attitude change, or will they need to take an extended break? Let's be clear. Sometimes the best thing you can do for your team and that individual is to send them home! If they aren't cooperating or doing their best to get on board, then you must think about what's best for other team members, the mission, and where you are trying to go at that moment.

I had a guy get super mad at another staff member. Had I not shown up when I did., there is no doubt fists would have been flying. I quickly pulled him to the side, got his side of the story, and took him away from everyone else to put him on "I.C.E."

- **Isolate:** Isolate the situation from harming themselves or others.
- **Communicate:** Let them communicate why they are so mad.
- **Explain:** Explain what's going to happen if they keep going down the current road of rage.

I followed the ICE protocol while he cooled down (pun intended) and then, out of left field, said, "Do you want a Gatorade?"

With a confused look, he said, "Uh, sure, ok."

What's so special about Gatorade, you ask? Nothing, but how are you going to stay mad at a guy that just gave you something for free? Trust me! It works every single time. People get tired, emotions take over, and sometimes you just need to let them go take a nap.

Elijah was running from Jezebel in the Old Testament (1 Kings 19) and asked God to take his life and just end it all! That's a deep and desperate request. God's response was to tell Elijah to take a nap and eat cake! I can completely get on board with those instructions!

After a Gatorade and a quick power nap, he was back on top and ready to apologize to the rest of the team and move forward. At that point, you can say to yourself, ladies and gentlemen, we've reached our cruising altitude. All attitudes are doing well and moving the mission forward. Change the batteries often and watch your mission stay energized and effective in all they do. When your atmosphere and attitude are in a good place, it makes communication much easier.

COMMUNICATE FOR YOUR CULTURE

Leadership is communication. It is communicating an array of things, but it is without a doubt the secret weapon of great leaders. Great leaders are great communicators. Communication is the lifeblood of culture. In the same way that blood flow keeps our human bodies alive, communication keeps culture alive. Anything that doesn't have blood flowing is dead. The communication we are talking about right now shouldn't be mistaken for stage presentations or someone who can give a great review at the annual board meeting. Communication takes place in much more than just words between humans. It is seen, heard, and even felt throughout our sphere of influence. Whether its thriving organizations, remote teams, or even strong families, I promise you the core of their culture will be communication.

> **GREAT LEADERS ARE GREAT COMMUNICATORS. COMMUNICATION IS THE LIFEBLOOD OF CULTURE.**

Culture is the way a group of people naturally talks, thinks, and acts. Culture is an important topic that leaders must understand; but in this book, we are focusing more on the elements that foster a great culture, and communication is one of them. Communication is the connecting bridge between information and action, just as a sky bridge would connect two tall skyscrapers in your nearest major city. If you don't have great communication, you will not have a great culture. Period. The end. Thanks for reading. Goodnight, world!

When we truly communicate, we are using the ability to translate thought into talk. It is the vehicle of your vision. It takes your ideas and turns them into inspirational conversations. Consider some of the greatest leaders the world has ever seen: they all worked hard and sacrificed in the name of leadership, but their greatest skill was their ability to communicate. Martin Luther King, Jr. could give a speech that would motivate anyone to action. President Ronald Regan had a long career of acting and ultimately understood that his ability to communicate would be the ticket to the presidency. Winston Churchill restored hope to an entire nation. Billy Graham filled stadiums so people could hear the message of the Gospel. Queen Esther spoke to one person, and it saved an entire race. When we speak, can move the minds of people from unconvinced to convinced.

COMMUNICATION IS THE CONNECTING BRIDGE BETWEEN INFORMATION AND ACTION.

Your leadership comes with the ability to create a culture with your words and your actions. How you utilize that will completely depend on you as a leader. Communication is found in many areas of our culture.

- Our tone
- Our body language

- Our decisions on policies and procedures
- Our focus and priorities

The central core of your culture will always be on display in the way communication happens. If I were starting a brand-new team today, right here, right now, here are the things I would focus on immediately to ensure we communicate well.

- **Create a common vocabulary:** Vocabulary should reflect the vision. Everyone should be saying the same thing. Are they teenagers or students? Clients or customers? If we are all trying to go the same way and are all here for the same mission, we must all speak the same language.
- **Construct communication channels:** Good teams are a tight group of people. We can probably even say they are friends. That's a very good thing! However, sometimes the communication lines can blur when there are multiple roles at play. As someone who works largely with family, this was a great challenge for us: are you speaking as my brother or my boss? Our solution was to assign different channels for specific roles. For example, we reserve texting and iMessage for personal, family, and friendship chatter; whereas work-related content goes through an application like Google Chat, Telegram, or Slack. If you are getting a phone call, it means I need your help. This might sound confusing at first, but I assure you that when everyone understands the different roads of communication to take, you'll arrive at your intended communication destination every time.

- **Commission a single source for official information:** The longest battle ever fought on the planet is the "He said, she said, they said" battle. In all my years, I have never met anyone named he, she, or they. Nothing will frustrate your team more than not having accurate information. Instead of suffering through group e-mail threads and paper agendas passed out at every meeting, consolidate official information in one location. We use an internal staff website that is administered by our Operations Department. If you are looking for official information like schedules, procedures, and organizational policies, you'll find it posted on the internal staff site. Whatever is in writing on the site trumps all other forms of conversation or communication. Everyone knows: it's not official until it's in writing on the staff site.

We have covered a lot about communication here, but I'll finish with probably the most important tip of them all. If you want to have excellent communication in your culture, give your mouth a break every once in a while and listen instead. If you listen, you will hear. You can sometimes gather more information just by listening to someone speak than you can by asking direct questions. At the end of the day, everyone wants to be heard.

Training the Troops

"We don't rise to the level of our expectations; we fall to the level of our training." Originally articulated by the Greek poet

Archilochus, this principle has been adapted and used by industries and organizations all over the world, none more than the Navy Seals. These instructors know that when pressure is turned up, people tend to cave. How do we fix that? Train, train, and train some more. Training a person to do a specific task in a specific way takes talent, one that few leaders possess.

LOVE THE PERSON, NOT ONLY THEIR PERFORMANCE.

Why is that? Most leaders want to spend so much time admiring the vision from the top of the mountain top that they do not know how to get back down to everyday life, where leading is walked out. Great leaders understand that to train someone effectively, they must ensure that the person can receive instruction, complete a skill, and report back in a timely and effective manner. Training people is truly getting them on track and helping them see how we are going to help them move forward in their own personal leadership journey. Here are some of the ways a leader may train people:

- **Hands-on:** A frequent routine of explanation, demonstration, and practice.
- **Content:** Classes, videos, articles, etc.
- **Experience:** A task or assignment is given to complete with little education on how to accomplish it.
- **Instructor-led:** Specific spaces designed to interact with participants over a structured set of information.

Every leader should be training a person in some shape or form. Training is where we learn the capacity of a person and what they have inside of them. You should always protect your own perspective of the person you are training. Training should never change the way you see or believe in them. If they do not get it right away, help them stick with it. They will come around, and it will exercise your ability to be patient. Love the person, not only their performance. People forget that some individuals (especially generation Z and beyond) need more training than just a thrown list of things to do. Each great leader should be training in four key areas:

- **Emotionally:** helping individuals develop and control their inner world
- **Relationally:** how people interact with other people
- **Professionally:** standards of excellence that support their craft
- **Spiritually:** the ability to be led by the Holy Spirit and know His voice

I do not know why the fitness world arrived at the concept of a "personal trainer" before every other industry, but that is exactly what great leaders do. They become personal trainers to help train in every area of a person's life. Although it is not flashy and fun all the time, leaders who care are leaders who train.

Success Scales

Every team wants to win, and in the eyes of our team, it is the leader who determines when we win. Celebrating success is a key factor in allowing growth to take place in your team. I like what Andy Stanley says: "What gets celebrated gets repeated." If we want our teams to grow, we have to tell them when they are doing something right. Momentum will naturally come with every win, and it's important that we celebrate those wins in a way that everyone gets acknowledged. How do we celebrate success? Here are some simple thoughts:

- **Stories:** When you come across a story of your mission being fulfilled because of someone on the team, tell it to everyone!
- **Showcase strategy:** Teams will come up with new tactics from time to time to improve results. (Remember the milestones in Part 1.) Use this opportunity to celebrate.
- **Stretch Their Limits:** Our role as a leader requires us to push people out of their comfort zone from time to time. When an individual or a team has been stretched, celebrate it in front of everyone. It validates to the team that the stretch was worth it, and it automatically ignites hope in others. They will begin to think, "Well, if they can do it, so can we."

Scale is a popular word in startup cultures, but the scale does not have to be solely focused on numbers. You can scale up efficiency or overall quality of communication or project management.

The final fact about teams here is that if people know when they are winning, they will want to win more. If they feel like they are losing, absent great leadership, there will be no motivation to do better the next time.

People join teams for two reasons:

- **To develop a vision**
- **To develop themselves**

Our part as the giver is to ensure that they are being celebrated when they accomplish either. I've always told people as they join the team that I would never try to hold on to them a day longer than they are supposed to be with us. My internal motto has always been, while they are mine, let me give them something that lasts them a lifetime. (To be clear, I realize that people aren't "mine" and more accurately assigned to the vision I'm leading at that given time. However, it rhymes, and we all know how preachers get with their rhymes, so here we are.)

I think building a team is one of the greatest parts of being a leader. The roster constantly changes, and you will be faced with new challenges with every person that crosses your path. As long as you keep the heart of a giver and make deposits into their life that make them better in what they love and who they are, you'll have a great legacy of leading teams, and that's a fact.

CHAPTER 18
MANTELS & MISSIONS
BUILDING TEAMS TO ACCOMPLISH AMAZING THINGS

Leading in a way that makes others want to lead themselves is the goal. If you are leading people correctly, you will find a time and space where you realize that they are leading you as much as you are leading them. That's the kind of team you want to have. You show up not to ask what they can do for you but with a plan for how you want to build them today. Building up people will forever be the most fulfilling part of your leadership journey. In the life of Jesus, He came for the mission of eternity and the training up of destiny. He was the example so others could follow in his footsteps. Now that we have team building, we need to focus on the individual areas of a person's life for which we are responsible for in our leadership.

When we talk about mantles and missions, we are talking about what it means to see the gift of leadership within a person and how to speak life to it and draw it out of them. Now everyone you come across may not be the next Billy

Graham, but they may be the next Billy the bus driver who spends 12 years of his life loving on a little guy who's afraid to go to school every day and yet grows up to change the world because he got a daily dose of confidence from his school bus driver.

When I think about my school years I remember all the teachers, principals, and instructors who believed in me more than I believed in myself.

> **SEE THE GIFT OF LEADERSHIP WITHIN A PERSON AND SPEAK LIFE TO IT.**

In the Old Testament, when Elisha started following Elijah's leadership, there was intense training that took place over ten years. Joshua followed Moses, and Peter followed Jesus. When you have someone that you know is willing and ready to respect the call of leadership in their life, training must take place before the launching of their leadership takes place.

Evangelist Reinhard Bonnke, of whom we spoke earlier, found his successor in Daniel Kolenda. It took ten years before he passed the reins of leadership to Daniel, who now is doing a phenomenal job leading Christ For All Nations.

Your gift of leadership to the next generation can be found when you truly train them in what they need for their journey; not just give them a chance to swing in the major leagues without first helping them develop their swing on the tee. How can we help people?

Corral Their Charisma

Charisma is contagious. It is fun to be around a person who's outgoing, says the right thing at the right time, and somehow appears to be just cruising through life without a care in the world. While this can be a great indicator of their interpersonal skills and potential for leadership, it doesn't mean they're ready to step straight into a position with no foundation. From time to time, help them develop other strengths by creating opportunities and events that are out of their comfort zone. It might be a different location for a day or two or shaking up the team by letting someone else take the lead for a week or so. This isn't punishment. It is a path to help them fully develop their leadership and prevent charisma from becoming a crutch. Charisma is a very charming and warm expression of a person; but if not managed properly, it can devolve into manipulation—or worse, deceit—and become cancerous to one's calling. We've seen hundreds of leaders fail in every area and industry simply because they thought they could coast through life on the charisma that God the Creator gave them. It starts with character.

Coach Their Character

"Charisma will get you there, but it is character that will keep you there." I love the accuracy of this quote. While I do not know where it originated, I've heard it said a million times from different people. Some get it, and others just use it for a good social media post. Character, like integrity, is the cornerstone of not only your life but your legacy. Character keeps you solid and allows your leadership a foundation to build upon because you have such a strong conviction of who you are when you're not leading. When you are training up a leader, recognize that they are still in training. They aren't going to get it perfect all the time, and mistakes are what make us stronger. We like to say, "You're not in trouble; you're in training." (Unless they really are in trouble, then that's a different story.) When deciding how to coach someone's character, it is important to ask this question: was that a lack of judgment or a lack of character? A lack of judgment is staying up the night before a big meeting you're presenting at because your favorite video game just released the next version. A lack of character is lying to your boss about why you were late to the meeting, unprepared, and didn't execute to the standard of excellence.

When we coach someone's character, we want to make sure that we paint a picture of the future for them without character. I like the way Dr. Henry Cloud teaches it: "Go hard on the issue. Soft on the person." Feed them a taste of truth with a sandwich of sanity. Start softly like a piece of bread, lay down the meat, and finish with love. You can speak the truth, in love, and really help people. Jesus came with grace and truth. You can have the grace of handling the conflict of their character softly while allowing the truth to take its rightful place, straight in their face. If you do not tell them the truth, who will? I hold for our teams what we call "Truth Thursday." It is a time set aside as needed to give people an opportunity to get things off their chest, or if I need to tell them something that might be a bit sensitive. By giving it a time and a specific office location, people know to come in braced a bit but knowing that in the end, it is only going to make them a better person and a better leader. Serve that sandwich of truth up daily and watch their character begin to truly develop. Every great athlete has a coach. A leader's character is no different. Coach them into better leadership performance, and everyone will win every time.

Keep Them Accountable

Leaders are rarely properly kept accountable. Accountability is so crucial in the life of leading someone else because you ultimately are creating and crafting something inside of that person that wasn't there before. It is easy to fall back on God-given charisma or lean into the strong character maybe their parents helped create, but to be accountable means that you are expecting something out of them; they may not be there yet. People need to be pushed. That's how we see greatness come from them. When we place accountability on someone, we are giving them the greatest vote of confidence we can because we realize there is more within them than they are performing within the current moment. How do we keep them accountable? Simple. Talk to them. It is the weekly text, the monthly meeting, and the quarterly catch-up. Making the effort to give time and attention to a person and help them navigate the areas they may be getting stuck in. I will add events to my calendar that say, "Check on John." If they report to you for work-related items, create a reporting rhythm that requires them to be responsible for certain information at a certain time.

When it comes to your finances, you have an accountant keep an account of what you have. Why do we resist having some keep an account of what we have to offer in our leadership? Let compassion lead this in your life. When you care about people truly getting better in their lives, it will naturally flow out of you.

Delegate Quickly

One way you can keep people accountable is by delegating things to them. I do not know why this is so hard for so many leaders to accomplish, but if anything is going to grow, it has to start with you, the one leading!

When we grow as leaders, so does everyone and everything around us. Delegation is the decision to grow. You do not have to delegate out an entire department. Start small and let it grow naturally.

I was developing a guy one time and gave him the assignment to unlock one door every morning at 7 a.m. Well, within a month, he had been late about 40% of the time, broke the key inside the door, and even completely forgot to tell anyone he was going to be out of town over an entire week! He did not understand the assignment!

However, over time he realized the importance of his role and even made his way up to a shift manager. Delegation requires people to dig deep into the places that demand better of themselves, and they always deliver. How can we help people win when we delegate? Give them the responsibility and the accompanying authority to go with it.

It has to be their thing from start to finish. I know they won't do it as great as you would, and they may not know how you like things done. If that's the case, then brush up on your communication and deliver instructions and vision in a way that can be captured so that they can succeed.

John Maxwell teaches that if a person can do the job 80% of the way, give it to them! Delegation develops them, and it gives you a chance to grow yourself.

Recognize the Gift

Yes, everyone can become a leader, as we've already covered, but I think there are people who are truly destined to lead great things, and it is our job to cultivate that calling on the inside of them and lead them down a path where they can discover their own purpose for themselves. These are the ones who catch your attention, impress you with their integrity, and show up when they do not have to. Those are the "hints of leadership" that show they've got the goods for greatness. In a session one time, I got up to talk about our television show, *Young Believer's Broadcast*, and invite the participants to consider supporting the show financially. After the session, a little boy came up to me and said, "I want to give this to help with the show." It was a crisp $100 bill. Although I was shocked that a twelve-year-old boy would have that in hand, I was also moved by his generosity, and recognized the gift of leadership in his life instantly. I found out his name was Cody, and I knew that Cody and I would do great things together for the kingdom of God. Years would come and go as he grew up, he would give a few weeks in his summer every year to intern, and right at the tail end of his high school career, he told me that he wouldn't be coming back for his final summer of the internship. I was very disappointed but quickly heard the familiar voice of the Lord, "Give him to me, and I'll give him back to you." Cody didn't come back right away, but I remember the day he showed up for Texas Bible Institute. He quickly got involved in everything and signed up for all the areas I was leading. It is one thing for you to recognize the gift of leadership in someone, but they must recognize it within you as well. Cody did that. He was always early to everything and showed up with extreme excellence in every way. He developed his leadership a little at a time, and after he graduated, we quickly hired him, where he completely skyrocketed with his leadership. During his time with us, he was the supervisor of three different departments, two of which he developed from the ground up; he was a part of our faculty and became a primary preacher during our summer camps. When Cody preaches, heaven shakes, and hell trembles. He has an amazing anointing on his life. I'm honored to be a very small part of Cody's journey. When people see him today, they are completely captivated by his charisma, humor, strength, and integrity. When I see Cody, I see all those things AND a little boy who had the tender heart of what great leadership is all about. There are many "Codys" around you. Look past your own leadership to find the gift within someone else, and develop it. God is sovereign, and every leader will find their path of purpose; but I do not want to be disobedient by failing to help someone else because I was too busy focusing on the wrong person: me. Recognize the gift. It will be your recognition of the gift in their life that sparks a chain reaction of greatness for their leadership and the leaders they lead. Greatness is a generational thing, and someone has to call them into the family.

Part Three
Leading | The Gifts

Leading is the daily action of gifting your leadership to people you have chosen to invest your life in. The first thing Jesus did was find a team of people that believed in the vision of the kingdom of Heaven, and in return, He believed in them.

I think Jesus's approach to the rhythms of His life is one all leaders should take note of and apply to their own leadership. Through the Gospels, we see stories of Jesus repeatedly doing three things:

- Spending private time for devotion, prayer, and rest
- Preaching and demonstrating the power of God to the crowds through public ministry
- Investing in the disciples for quality, intentional teaching, and training

I can understand wanting to spend time with God and speaking on stages to people but slowing things down to invest and train twelve guys took me some time to figure out. Then I realized the purpose of leadership is to give your gifts to the people you are leading. Jesus understood that He could put the disciples on a fast track that would help them become who they were called to be simply by *giving* them the *gifts* He already had.

We all receive gifts that we enjoy and never want to depart from, but in the life of a leader, the giving of your gifts is what makes leadership so fulfilling. When you *re-gift* something that is special to you, you give it to someone you know will appreciate it the way you did. When a leader is leading, they are giving the gifts they have for the purpose of developing another person.

When you are leading, you are giving. How do you know if you are leading? Listen to the questions. If the questions are normally about the day-to-day operations of what you do, then more relationships may be needed before someone is ready to receive your gift. But when you receive a question about a life situation or they ask you about your beliefs on a topic, you know you're in a position to recognize who is willing to receive the gifts you have to give.

Leading with your gifts will take internal motivation and a methodical structure to your management style. Sometimes, it is implied that leaders and managers should be considered separate roles. I beg to differ! They are not separate roles but rather separate responsibilities. I am a husband and a father, and those responsibilities do not change the fact that I'm one man. When you are leading, you should be leading and managing through whatever is before you. If you have a group project with a bunch of volunteers to paint the church nursery, leading will involve conversation on why it's important to have a place that's safe and welcoming to first-time mothers. Managing would focus on things like having enough equipment ready to go so when the team shows up, you aren't wasting people's time waiting for supplies.

The gifts we are going to cover in this final part are a select few of a much larger library. However, I believe when a leader leads with these specific gifts, it will make a lasting impact on individuals and the team. Whether we realize it or not, the team desires *decisions* and *consistency*. They value authentic *time* with leadership and want new *opportunities* to hone their professional skills but are mindful that *pace* is important in their ever-changing lives.

Knowing everything we've covered up to this moment, remember you have a *gifting* and you are a *giver*, so let's give these *gifts*.

CHAPTER 19
DECISIONS
DOMINOS AND PUZZLES

Marriage is a beautiful thing and equally brutal if both individuals aren't willing to show up for the relationship. What's the hardest part about marriage, you ask? That's easy, deciding where to eat! It is not that we are always in a tug-o-war about where we are going to land: it is the process of deciding.

Leaders are in the same boat! Leaders have to make decisions. It is an action that only your leadership can carry out. The level of the decision will be your choice based on the level of management you prefer. I've never really played the game of dominos very well; so instead of playing, I like to watch world record holders set up hundreds of thousands of dominos and then watch them fall into perfect place as Will Smith did in *Collateral Beauty*. When a leader decides, that decision is converted into a domino in the grand setup of your teams and systems. They place people on the right path of purpose and productivity. No longer are people just aimlessly waiting around for productive things to do; now, they have a plan. When decisions are made, it is a gift to those you are leading. The process of deciding can be scrutinized and formalized, but it is a part of every leader's skill set that has to be developed. With decision comes peace and a determination to accomplish what you decided.

In March of 2020, the world as we knew it changed when COVID-19 became a household and boardroom word. When you're a part of a Christian ministry whose primary role is to gather large crowds of church groups, offer residency for college students, and meet weekly in a large church venue, the last thing you want to hear is that there's a virus that spreads rapidly due to people being in close proximity with each other. I'd like to take just a moment and walk you through what we decided to do when the COVID-19 virus showed up at our doorstep and how those decisions became the dominos our teams needed. In comparison, every organization and business had to walk through the same uncertainties. These are the events that took place.

We had just completed our third retreat of about 800 guests, and information about this fast-spreading virus was beginning to pick up steam. In times of crisis or panic, I look to organizations similar to ours for guidance in making decisions. Our local and regional governmental offices hadn't said much, nor did the school districts, but one organization had made a drastic call that put the whole city on notice: the Houston Rodeo and Livestock show had officially been canceled. That's when I knew this thing was serious.

This annual event referred to by Texans as simply "the Rodeo" is one of the largest things that happens all year long in our metroplex. Over a twenty-day period, 2.6 million people will attend the Houston Livestock Show and Rodeo. It is staffed by 33,000 volunteers and contributes almost $500 million to the local economy. Just nine days into the 2020 season, the Houston Rodeo had been canceled due to the spreading virus. If the rodeo was being shut down, either we needed to take this seriously, or Jesus was coming soon! (He either is or has based upon when you're reading this.) I knew that if we didn't make *decisions* across our organization quickly, we were going to be forced to, and chaos would commence quickly.

When leaders make decisions, it takes the guesswork out for the team and closes off the open loop for aimless and unproductive conversation or speculation to spread among the team. I called an immediate and impromptu meeting for the board of directors, and we made decisions that were going to be difficult but beneficial for the safety of our staff and students, the guests we serve, and the bottom line of the organization. Good leaders make decisions that benefit them. Great leaders make decisions that benefit others. After deciding that these decisions could affect us for a few weeks, we made the decision not to hold in-person programs across all outreaches of the organization, and in-house residency would not be available for the foreseeable future. We made this decision on a Thursday night at about 6:30 p.m. and put our Communications team on notice for Friday morning announcements. Communication sequence is crucial if you want a smooth delivery of information. The last thing you want is an announcement that went out via email, and the people answering the phones in the office have no idea what you're talking about. The team prepared a statement that went to the staff at 7:00 a.m., parents & participants at 8:00 a.m., and announced in the classrooms at 9:00 a.m. Campuses were cleared and closed by 12:00 noon.

Our church family congregation was put on notice later that Friday that we would be exclusively offering an online experience for the upcoming Sunday. Now our teams had 48 hours to pull off a great online service simply because a decision had been made with enough time to act on it.

As we got a week or two past these decisions, we realized that other organizations were following in our footsteps, and even the local and state officials began to put executive orders in place that would have caused us to make some of the same moves just a few days later. The length of these orders required two rounds of furloughs, and we adjusted our program calendar for the next two years; each day was a day that required fresh decisions and fresh faith.

Your decisions today will determine your destiny tomorrow. Decisions set the course in uncertain times and through unknown terrain.

> **YOUR DECISIONS TODAY WILL DETERMINE YOUR DESTINY TOMORROW.**

When all the decisions have been set up like dominos, then the people around you can watch all the details fall into place one piece at a time. Unlike a puzzle, though, decisions made by leadership set the course that then allows your team time to figure out what the new vision looks like and how it is all going to fit together.

Think of it this way: Leaders set up dominos. Teams solve puzzles.

- Decisions give guidance to the lost.
- Decisions give peace to the uncertain.
- Decisions drive productivity.
- Decisions communicate clarity.
- Decisions create a platform that other people can walk on.
- Decisions settle inaccurate assumptions.

One great leader I know would always say in times of question, "Here's what we're going to do." When you heard those words, you knew there was no more debate, no more talking about it, no more wondering. This was an announcement to everyone in the room that a decision had been made. When leaders make decisions, we inject confidence into those we are leading that build the bravery needed to move things forward.

So, if decisions are so important, how do we make them? I mentioned earlier there was a process and sometimes even a formula for making decisions, but let's start with the most important factor in making your decisions: listening to the Holy Spirit! We say it all the time, "The Holy Spirit knows everything, and the Holy Spirit is always right." When you make a choice to listen to the voice of God on a matter, the next step is simply obeying those instructions. Bible school students used to ask me, "What's the most important thing I can learn while I'm here?"

My answer never wavered, "How to hear the voice of God."

By hearing the spirit speak, you never have to question or rely on your own abilities to make the decision alone. My brother-in-law David said it best: "If your decision doesn't feel right, it's probably not." Proverbs 3:5 is a leader's best friend. "Trust in the Lord with all your heart and *lean not on your own understanding…"* In other words, do not make decisions alone. Proverbs 11:14 says in a "multitude of counsel" there is safety. Having great and godly voices around you can help in hearing wisdom from the experience of others. Decisions are the driving force behind any kind of progress. Like a plant thirsty for water, so is the person waiting for a solid decision. When I asked Amanda to marry me, although I was confident in her expected response, the time waiting to hear her **decision** felt like an eternity! Thankfully, she said, "YES!"

There was a day when people made decisions for you; and then one day, you made them for yourself. Be the kind of leader that protects people from making bad decisions and be willing to let go when they make decisions you disagree with. Decisions are a gift from the leaders in your life that are worth re-gifting to others.

You honor the people you are leading when you make decisions that will give them time to process, turn that decision into a domino, and watch it fall perfectly into the plan full of purpose.

CHAPTER 20
CONSISTENCY
STAYING IN TUNE WITH THE TRUTH

As a musician, I've played multiple instruments in all kinds of bands. I was in the marching band in high school, played jazz piano in college, participated in choirs at the state level, and even did three semesters of musical theater. Not to mention the thousands of hours of praise and worship teams I've played on, sang on, and ran the lyrics for on those old school transparency machines before computers generated the lyrics on a screen. Music was all around me for as long as I can remember, and one thing I know about music is that whatever you are doing, whether playing an instrument or singing with your voice, you have to stay in tune with the people you're playing with if you want to sound good. Tuning is a unique thing, and I'm fascinated by the science behind it as well. To match the pulsating frequency of a specific note, the sound wave must be sped up or slowed down, so it is vibrating at a specific rate that matches the intended note. Nothing is worse than someone who doesn't know that they are singing out of tune or playing in a completely wrong key. Just go to YouTube and search "worship fails" for some great laughs. Do not worry; we aren't laughing AT people. We are laughing WITH them. If you've been in any kind of church music for an extended period of time, you've had those moments that could easily place you in those videos too. Why is tuning so important? It all comes down to consistency.

Consistency is something great leaders show up with every day. It is given to the teams they lead. It is used to keep themselves accountable, and it is a lesson worth passing on to others. A consistent leader is a confident leader. When someone is consistent, they are someone you can count on. Someone you can trust and someone that you know will get the job done. When I want to make sure I or those I am leading are being consistent, I simply ask, "How's your tuning?" or "Do you need to check your tuning?" Let's break this down a bit more because I think it adds so much value to all leaders.

A CONSISTENT LEADER IS A CONFIDENT LEADER.

As a guitar player, you've got six strings that all have to be in tune with one another in order to sound right. Now, sure, we can get into all kinds of crazy tunings out there like my childhood hero SCC (shout out to Steven Curtis Chapman). But for the sake of this illustration, I'm going to stick with standard tuning. For those who do not play the guitar, each string is one single note when plucked. As you pluck each of the six strings, you will get the five notes of one octave and one note from the next: E, A, D, G,

B, E. When I want to check consistency tuning as a leader, I run the list of these strings.

- E: Emotions
- A: Appearance
- D: Desires
- G: God
- B: Body
- E: Eternity

Let's pluck these strings one by one, shall we?

Emotions

Emotions are the greatest driving force of a leader's mental and productive state. Either you will manage your emotions, or your emotions will manage you. It is your choice. Emotions aren't a bad thing; they are actually a God thing. God created these emotions so we could have great freedom when it comes to experiencing life. However, when your emotions are out of tune, you make bad decisions, your motives and intentions do not always sync up with your values, and you tend to do and say things you typically wouldn't. A great leader knows how to keep their emotions in check while they are leading. When a leader's emotions are in tune, they are poised and positioned to address whatever is in front of them with clarity that can be trusted. Is it ok for leaders to feel things? Absolutely! I'd be scared if you didn't!

There's a time and place for everything; God teaches us that in Ecclesiastes 3. If you get some bad news or something that makes you angry during the staff meeting, it is not the time to unleash your Hulk-like wrath on everyone at the table. Be consistent in how you process your soul. Have a time and place to go and work through what you're feeling. This is a good place where Christian counseling may really benefit you and your leadership. I've had seasons where great and godly Christian counselors have walked me through questions and emotions that would have taken me much longer to navigate had I done it myself. If your emotions are in tune, chances are the others will quickly follow.

Appearance

Appearance is everything from your clothes to what you post online for the entire world to see. Leaders are people that are esteemed and sometimes even revered. They represent a set of values and a vision that is being built in and around other people. If you show up to a meeting that you are hosting dressed to the nines but show up to someone else's morning class looking like a bum in your sweats, there is no consistency. Again, there is a time and place for everything. In our organization, like many other companies, we have a dress code for our attire that we require employees to uphold. Why? We value consistency, and by keeping your appearance consistent, you will naturally keep other areas of your life consistent too.

I've been doing remote work long before it was forced upon the world with the pandemic. Every productivity specialist will always tell you that if you want to be productive at home, you have to start your day by getting dressed. It puts your mental state in a place of productivity. When you walk into a nice restaurant or a hotel, and you see an employee dressed well and put together, you immediately say to yourself, "They have answers. They can help me with my problem." That's what keeping your appearance in tune does for you and those around you. There have been moments where people are changing their hair and hair color every ten seconds. I'm not against that, but you must take into consideration how that will affect your consistency as a leader. Yes, there will always be a place to dress casually, even lounge around in comfortable clothes, but when you are leading, people think twice about your presentation if you just throw on your favorite "chill mode clothes."

Desires

Desires determine your destiny. There are great godly desires, and then there are desires that distract you from what you are assigned to do. Every season of life has a focus. If you are in college, graduating should be your focus, not the continual parties that de-rail academics. When we check our tuning around our desires, we simply ask ourselves, "Will this keep me focused on this season?" Desires are like appetites. You can grow appetites or starve them.

Grow the desires that develop you for your destiny and starve the ones that you know will distract you. If staying up too late at night on an endless scroll of pointless social media posts is causing you to be anxious because you have not "arrived yet," turn off your phone. Leave it in another room or even your car, so you can focus on what you're supposed to at night: sleep. Normally, if you find yourself wanting more attention, seeking selfish rewards, or desiring a spotlight, it is more than likely being influenced by what you are allowing into your life. There have been times when I need to turn *positive* voices in my life *down* simply because they are stirring something up in me that gives me a desire to go faster, work harder, be better, and try to do everything in my own might. The Bible is pretty clear: "Not by might nor by power, but by My Spirit" (Zechariah 4:6). Stay consistent in what you desire, and your destiny will develop before your very eyes because He that began a GOOD work (that's in you) is faithful to complete it. (Phil 1:6)

God

It is crazy to think that we would need to be consistent with God, but like any relationship in our life, He deserves our attention, too. So many times, we want a word from God, but He just wants a consistent word from us. When you decide to build your life and leadership on the faith of believing that God is in charge, you quickly move from discipleship to lordship. It is the one key factor that makes your entire relationship change for the better. When we are consistent with our relationship with God, something special happens, and our desires change.

In the guitar world, sometimes, you will play two strings back and forth to ensure that everything is staying in tune as you go down the guitar. The desire string will absolutely point to the God string, and vice versa. If your desires are off, more than likely, your consistency with God is off too.

I ask young leaders all the time, "How are things with Jesus?" Every so often, I will get an honest answer from someone saying, "They could be better." To me, that is the best news because I know if they are honest with me, they can be honest with God. He is such a loving Father who cares about your well-being. "For God so loved…." is how John 3:16 starts, after all! When your relationship with God is strong, you will hear things for your life and for the people you are leading too. Keeping consistent in your relationship with the Holy Spirit is the best way to keep your edge as a leader. I asked a great Pastor that I admired one time, "How do you keep your edge as a leader?"

"Pray in the Holy Ghost, and when you're done praying, pray some more!" he said without hesitation.

In other words, keep your relationship with God consistent. I believe that we are anointed and assigned to help people with their relationship with Jesus. A great leader in your life will constantly point you back to your ever-growing relationship with your Abba Father. Keep it consistent. Keep it in tune.

Body

This body that you are currently in is your vehicle for the assignment. You would take care of a rented vehicle or something that someone else owns. Well, that is exactly the scenario here. Sometimes when we hear leadership stuff about health, we tend to think we have to be this chiseled bodybuilder to properly take care of our bodies. I think optimal health is a good thing and something we should all strive for, my friend Xavier constantly reminds me: progress over perfection.

Isn't that being consistent? Showing up and doing what you must do to finish the job shows your consistency. When it comes to staying in tune with our body, it means just that! Know your body and know what to do when it gets off a little bit.

For me, I can tell when I've had too much sugar. It affects my sleep, and if my sleep is thrown off, I'm guaranteed to have the spirit animal of the Grinch the following day. This means my interactions with my wife and kids will not be the best, and that will extend into meetings with the teams. Poor decisions will be made, and in six weeks, I will be asking: "Who made that stupid decision? Only to find out it was me, myself, and I."

Being consistent in your body means that you are caring for it at the best level you can, so it will care for you. Good hygiene, proper balanced nutrition, regular movement, and restful sleep are all things that keep you consistent as a leader. You can tell instantly between someone who takes care of themselves and someone who does not. That is not motivation; it is consistency.

Eternity

Every day we get up, we lead, we develop people, but for what purpose? Yes, there are wonderful natural reasons that make life on earth day to day a wonderful thing, but in the light of eternity, what does it matter? Christians believe the Bible when it says that eternity is a real thing, and it is an ongoing, never-ending, forever existence. As a leader, I want to do things that matter for eternity's sake, not simply my quarterly report. It can be so easy to get caught up in the hustle and bustle of everything that we forget what really matters.

That little phrase "in the light of eternity" keeps my thinking consistent with the idea that forever is longer than today…simple, but potent. Do not let your leadership get flustered with things that won't live past sunset. If someone does you wrong, forgive them. If you have to spend a week more than expected on a project, take the week. It will not make everything fall apart. The thought of eternity causes you to zoom out, keeps your mindset consistent with Scripture, and reminds you to *make every breath count* for a viewpoint bigger than yourself. One day we will hear those words, "Well done, good and faithful servant!" How do we become faithful? Consistency.

Consistency counts. Consistency keeps us constant and constantly keeps us concrete. Concrete leaders are solid people. Great leaders understand that consistency counts in your life personally today, or it will ripple down and affect your team in a week. If you ignore it, the entire organization could feel it six months from now. Consistency is what keeps us moving.

People love to know their leaders are consistent. They have predictable patterns that set them apart from every other person in their life. That is why we trust leaders so much: because we can count on them. Some of the greatest leaders I know simply answer their phones. If I call them, they consistently pick up. I never feel like I am intruding. I always feel welcomed. They are consistent in their conversation and counsel. When I think about a gift I want to re-gift to others I lead, consistency will always make that list.

> **CONSISTENCY KEEPS US CONSTANT AND CONSTANTLY KEEPS US CONCRETE. CONCRETE LEADERS ARE SOLID PEOPLE.**

CHAPTER 21
TIME
YOU MANAGE TIME: IT DOES NOT MANAGE YOU

Time. We all have the same amount every single day and every single week. No one gets more, and no one gets less. In the life of a leader, it is the most valuable gift you could give. When you give your time, you are automatically not giving your time somewhere else.

For decades, people have employed time management principles in an attempt to accomplish more. I think these (coupled with energy management) can be extremely effective, the end goal of any kind of time management should lead in one of two directions: seed or harvest. There's a biblical principle that we see sewn into the fabric of scripture known as a seed, time, and harvest. When you plant a seed, you can expect a harvest. Seems simple right? If I plant a lemon seed, I will get a lemon tree, but not overnight. It is going to take what? Time. Time is the bridge between seed and harvest. What a leader does with their time demonstrates where their values and priorities live. When you make a life-giving decision about what you will do with your time, you are honoring God for the gift of time itself, and you are planting a seed into something to obtain harvest later.

In 2009, I saw this gift of time worked masterfully by a leader I admire named Terry Storch. Terry is a technologist who has chosen to use his life for expanding the kingdom of God via technology. I was on a trip to Tulsa, Oklahoma, and my schedule opened up so I had an extra day before flying home. I knew that I was semi-close to this church that was making huge waves in the tech space around that time.

Back then, they were called LifeChurch.tv, now known as Life.Church. Where many people know and love the leadership and teaching of Pastor Craig Groeschel (as I do, which you know by the number of quotes you've seen thus far), fewer know some of the people behind the scenes. Terry is one of those guys. I had met Terry once briefly in Nashville but had no real relationship with him any reason for him to take me seriously. With a cold e-mail, I told him I was in the area and planned to drive over and see the church and would love to connect again if he had time. To my shock and surprise, he responded and agreed, and we set a time to meet. Time is an anchor in your assignment. I got in the rental car and traveled the ninety minutes southeast to Edmond, Oklahoma, where Life.Church's central offices are.

For the entire morning, Terry graciously gave me a tour of not only his area but of the entire church. We would walk down hallways while he explained what everything was and why they decided to do things the way they did, and then he would stop walking every so often and ask me questions about my life, dreams, and the visions of things I wanted to see accomplished with my own life. He never rushed; he was extremely present. If the entire Old Testament was offline for users in Europe in the You Version Bible App that Terry oversees, I surely didn't know it. After a gracious tour, he asked if I had time for lunch. I did, and over our meal, he continued to answer question after question that I threw his way. He never was flustered or made me feel like I was wasting any of his time. It was a memorable experience for me and one that I remember almost fifteen years later. To this day, if I reach out to Terry for questions on new technology or thoughts on which way we should develop our systems, he's always kind to respond. Terry is a vulnerable leader, and he even takes the time to write a weekly dispatch from his own website, multiplying value of what he's learning, reading, and observing in life by sharing it with others.

Time is a gift great leaders give to the people they believe in.

TIME IS A GIFT GREAT LEADERS GIVE TO THE PEOPLE THEY BELIEVE IN.

Many times we think that leaders forget about us or they are too busy to truly develop us. Be careful with that thought process. When a leader gives you an opportunity to do something, they are giving you time on their dime to develop yourself. Recognize that when a leader gives you a piece of their time, they are giving you more than just seconds, minutes, and hours. Time is an expression of their life and what they have walked through. Let's take some time and look at it.

Experience

Chances are, the person you are considering a leader at this moment is older than you and has more experience than you. Time spent sharing those experiences is the greatest gift they can give you. What took them ten years to learn, they can download to you in ten minutes. Experience comes at a price to someone. It either shows up with the one who paid the price or by the person who has made their way through multiple experiences and figured it out along the way. Both approaches are acceptable. No matter how much time you have with this leader, realize that every moment matters. More is caught than taught. If that's accurate, since it is not their responsibility to teach it, it becomes your responsibility to catch it.

Leaders who have experienced things can hear things in smaller sentences and have a whole snapshot of where you've come from and where you are headed. In a moment of some IT trouble one time, I picked up the phone and called a friend who was successful in the IT space. He created database systems and structures that would run up to two million rows of data a second.

For all the nerds out there, you know that's smoking fast! After about five minutes of explaining the past five hours of the network issues we were having, he gave a suggestion that took about five seconds to say and five minutes to implement, and it worked!

An experienced ear knows how to hear for the clues and the context of the problem and then give value to help you find a solution. Leaders who are willing to give you their time really do have the heart to help.

Heart to Help

Compassion is at the core of every great leader, as we've already discussed at the beginning of the book. There is a desire to make things better, to make people better, and to find solutions to seemingly impossible tasks.

They will always go the extra mile for people when they are willing to give time. They come in early to write that recommendation letter for you and stay late for the impromptu conversation someone asked them to have. They are first to pick up the bill at lunch and last to ask for any help. They simply want to serve. When someone has the heart to help like that, they truly are modeling being the hands and feet of Jesus. If you find a leader who is willing to help you by giving you their time, recognize and respect that you have found a great leader.

A Different Perspective

Sometimes the best thing you can get is a different perspective from a different person. If all your friends, family, and counselors are drawing from the same well, you are going to have a very mediocre and boring life. Different perspectives mean that people see the same thing from a different angle. When you see something differently, you could speak from a different place, and it is from those different places that you hear and see different things. When you hear what someone has to say, you are multiplying your time by basing it on the time they've already invested in the matter. Do not be afraid of hearing a different perspective. It might be the thing you need to point you in a new direction.

Time Is a Treasure

Like finding lost treasure, so is the power of understanding your time and how it will serve you on a day-to-day basis. Studies have shown that the people who are typically the most productive and the most successful are people of incredible routine. They measure their time to the minute and realize that when they invest time, it is not coming back to them, so they invest wisely.

How do you invest time? You commit it to something of value. This value will be different for everyone, but it will always result in you feeling better about life and your circumstances around what you're trying to accomplish.

Amanda is so amazing at reminding me of some advice she gave me at the beginning of our marriage. I was having one of those days where the calendar was packed back-to-back. I knew it was going to be a fast-paced day. I taught a class, had videos to film, a few in-person meetings, and I was even going to try and squeeze in a walk through a new construction site we were building.

It was such a crazy day (a schedule I would never attempt today) that I had even reached out to every person the day before saying, "It is a really full day for me, and if you could please be ready and on time to ensure my other appointments do not fall behind, I'd appreciate it."

I felt good. Everyone was in the know, and I was ready to go! As it happened, appointment two took longer, the lighting kit broke during the video shoot, and I was super frustrated. I texted my wife give her a heads up about my emotional state and what she had to look forward to with my call once I got on the commute. Her wise and soft reply said, "You manage time. Time doesn't manage you."

That quick reminder from a simple text message gave me the perspective to take off my leadership hat, enlarge my pastoral heart and just talk to the guys on the crew while we were waiting for some spare parts. In those moments, I heard things from their heart, got to impart some ideas to them, and later, one guy told me in all the years of being around me, it was the greatest conversation and brought the most value to his life. Had I not recognized (thanks to Amanda) that I had the time to do something different than the prescribed daily schedule, I may have missed a great opportunity to invest my time into those guys.

Learning how to manage your time and truly treasuring it is an art form that takes time in and of itself, but if you were to sit down and list out the things that fuel you, you're going to come up with a great list rather quickly. For me, driving in the car, being with my wife and our boys, enjoying great coffee from a third-wave coffee shop, tinkering around with technology and different software hacks, and playing musical instruments are just a few things that fuel me.

In leadership, you must stay full if you're going to be able to pour. You can't give what you do not have. Allotting proper time for recreation is a really important step in keeping your leadership cup full. I read in a book once that "Recreation is just a re-creation of fuels for your mission." Time is a treasure that will bring you great value when you recognize what it is truly worth.

For the remainder of this chapter, we are going to talk about tips and tricks you can use when managing time and making sure you are managing time, and it is not managing you.

⏰ TIME TIPS ⏰

Calendar Curation

The calendar is a map of your time. You show me your calendar (even if you do not put things on it), and I will show you what you value in life. Michael Hyatt's famous quote, "What gets calendared gets done." is a mantra for every leader who wants to take their time seriously. Whether it is digital or paper, by capturing your intentions of what you want to do with your time, you are making a commitment to yourself and announcing to others that these are the places and people you're going to give your most valuable resource to. Though we could completely nerd out on a million and one little calendar hacks and productive practices, I'll point you toward some other great resources that have already done a phenomenal job breaking downing these methods. *Redeeming Your Time* by Jordan Raynor is a solid start into the deep waters of productivity power with a perspective that is biblically-based and incredibly practical. However, I will still give you three of my favorite tips that I believe will help you crush the time monster that tries to plague us all.

Time Blocks

Time blocks build up your days brick by brick. While this isn't a complicated or new concept, it is overlooked by many. The basic idea is that you create a block of time focused on a specific type of activity. You may take your morning and split it into three different blocks. For me, I am a recovering night owl converted to a morning bird (I prefer to be a blue jay or a lark), and my mornings are precious to me and my productivity. An example of some blocks could look like the following:

5am - 6:30am | Health & Fitness
7:00am - 9:00am | Family & Food
9:30 - 11:30 | Administration Tasks (E-mail, Documents, Calendaring, Etc.)

By splitting your day into blocks, you are keeping all the like tasks and activities together at the same time. You may have a block for playtime with your kids or a block every Friday where you just call someone to catch up and see how things are in their world. People love to talk, and as a pastor, I have good news for them: I love to talk too!

Sometimes, though, we need more time than is possible on a Sunday morning. By creating a weekly time block, you can maintain a consistent rhythm for keeping conversations fresh, because the people change frequently.

I used to use Wednesday night dinner as my block for people who wanted to catch up or pick my brain on something. I usually picked the same restaurant, and every other Wednesday or so, I'd show up with a new person ready for a great conversation.

It didn't change my weekly rhythm, and I didn't go back and forth multiple times looking for the best available time; the blocking did it for me. I have Tuesday morning via Zoom or Wednesday for dinner, your choice!

Blocking helps you see your day visually, and with all the great calendar applications out there now, you can really get a grasp on where your time is going.

Themed Days

Themed days ran across my path originally from a someone you've already met in this book, Mr. Mike Vardy. The idea is simple yet powerful in that each day we have a type of cumulative work we are trying to accomplish. If you know that meetings in the office require you to be dressed a certain way and you won't be taking any phone calls, then theme your day in a way where all of your meetings land on Monday. This really does change the game because then you are free to allow the other areas of your week to focus on different tasks and environments.

For example, if Monday is meeting day in the office and Tuesday is admin day for reports and spreadsheets, then you do not need to dress up in a suit and tie and may be able to accomplish that work from a coffee shop. If Wednesday becomes "Writing Wednesday" (as I've coined it for myself), then I do not want to talk, see, or hear anyone or anything on that day so I can focus on writing. Now I know this may be difficult for you if you aren't in charge of your own schedule; however, maybe you start it on the weekends. Maybe you have a "rest day" for your Sabbath and then a "reset day" where you mow the lawn, run errands, and restock the pantry for the week. Knowing what is on the radar of your life helps you manage your time by being able to reflect and prepare for what's coming.

Super Batching

This one gets a little into the pro-space of the productivity world, but it can be very simple to integrate into your day-today rhythms. The idea is simple in that most days and weeks; you have the same kinds of tasks to complete. Phone calls to schedule doctor's appointments for the kids, return your grandma's call, etc. Instead of scattering all those phone calls throughout the whole day or week, you are going to batch them together and do all the calls in one sitting at a single time. This works great for errands, admin-type tasks, podcast recording, you name it!

One way to track it is using a method described in David Allen's *Getting Things Done*, among others. On your list of things you want to accomplish (need to do or want to do), add a hashtag to that line item. "Go to store #errand," "Call grandma. #phone" By adding the hashtag, you are adding context to the task and later can re-visit and focus on one hashtag at a time. Most of the popular applications out there, like Todoist, Notion, Asana, Omni Focus, etc., will allow you to filter lists by contexts or labels. This gives you the clearest picture of your context in a list that might seem a bit overwhelming. The nice thing about contexts, too, is they are very flexible. Some examples may include contexts around energy levels, tools you need to accomplish the job (computer, tablet, phone), or even how long the task will take (5min, 30min, 90min). There's plenty of writing out there about batching, and it will quickly supercharge your time management. Okay, you did good! The nerd sequence is complete. Let's get back to time….

The Harvest of Time

Time can be taken. Time can be given. Time can be multiplied, but the most important thing we can do with it is turn it into a seed for something greater in the future. Every morning you wake up should be an announcement to yourself that you have time to sow into something special today. We aren't promised tomorrow, and how we sow that time today will affect every area of our lives in the future. If you overwork today, you will be burnt out tomorrow. If you ignore your spouse, you'll lack connection and intimacy. If you spend a decade pushing past activities and events with your kids, you will wake up when they graduate high school with no relationship or awareness of who they are becoming as an adult, because you didn't sow your time wisely. On the opposite side of this biblical principle is the wonderful word "harvest." Harvesting is that joyous process of gathering everything that is now ready to be enjoyed! It is a confirmation that the time has been used effectively and wisely. Harvest happens when we sow seeds wisely and give them the time they need to grow properly. Give the gift of time, and watch it come back to you with added value for your life and your vision. Watch it return in a person whose life is flourishing with a great marriage, family, work ethic, and emotional health, all because you were willing to sow the seed of time.

Harvest doesn't happen without intention, and it requires time. When you re-gift your time for the enrichment of others, you give the world another example of what great leadership is all about.

CHAPTER 22
OPPORTUNITY
OPEN DOORS LEADS TO OPEN ROADS

Opportunity is the open door to your leadership development. Life can't be done solo. It requires a tribe of people to help us reach the places we've been called to. The entire foundation of this book can really be traced back to this one word.

Everyone wants opportunities. It is a chance for change. A place to prove what you have to offer to the world. It even provides a sense of security knowing that someone is willing to train you and help you get to where you want to go in life. We place such a high value on opportunities in our culture that we use the word interchangeably with other words in the dictionary. For example, we do not have problems in our organization. We have "opportunities" to find a solution and make it better. Where that may be extreme for some, I realize the power that comes when an opportunity is in front of you, and you jump into it with both feet. Over this chapter, I want to give you four examples of where you will see opportunity in your life and how you can apply it when you are leading. Though out your leadership, you will experience:

- The opportunity of observation
- The opportunity to own
- The opportunity of oversight
- The opportunity of offering

Before I explain each of these, you need to see them all play together in a portion of my life story. Let me walk you through some of the different seasons of my media career and then hit rewind to explain these valuable areas and how opportunity can and will affect you.

As a twelve-year-old homeschooled kid who wasn't too interested in the everyday subjects of math, science, and history, I found myself in the office of Clayton Miller. Clayton was on staff with my parents and primarily did art and design; but in his free time, he would crank up this little program called Adobe Premiere Pro 4.0. It was video editing software that let you edit video footage on your own computer! Nowadays, that sounds silly since you can do everything with your phone, but in the late 90s, this was a big deal. I would sit and watch Clayton edit videos for hours. Seeing my interest in media, my mother convinced Clayton to do some projects with me to help me get started. We did some early green screen things and even created an intro video for one of the upcoming events we hosted that lasted seven seconds! It was so short that we decided to play it twice because the audience missed it the first time. Clayton gave me an opportunity to just sit there and watch him do what he loved to do. He gave me an opportunity to discover a thing I loved while he was doing the thing he loved. Opportunity is a gift that leaders give to those they believe in.

Years later, we had started a television show called *Young Believer's Broadcast*. We had hired this overpriced production company to come in twice a year, film a ton of shows at a time, and then take it back to the "big city" and produce our vision. As a guy who was just a college kid, I saw the product these guys were producing and quickly said,

"I know I could do just as good, if not better than this!"

After finding out what we were paying these guys, the challenge to do it better and for a better price boiled up inside of me. My dad made an agreement with me that I could make my own show, and we would do an A/B test side by side with the "professionals." If there was no difference in quality or content, I could start producing the show. There it was: my moment to make a difference and *own an opportunity*! I ended up passing the test and went on to produce the show for nearly ten years. YBBtv was a show created and written with young adults in mind. So often, Christian Media (which I believe in) for that age group was created to be very evangelistic. This is needed. However, we wanted to provide a show that was driven by discipleship and education about our faith and how to live a life based on the Holy Bible. It was our effort to provide digital discipleship in a vast sea of programming. My mission was simple: produce a great show that networks would want to carry! After developing the show, we had to find distribution, and I quickly found myself in the world of the NRB.

The National Religious Broadcasters Association has been

around for more than 70 years, and its mission is to support and represent the legal rights of Christian communicators and broadcasters in the United States. I met many people through the NRB that were instrumental in helping us get YBBtv off the ground, but none more than Phil Cooke.

I think his bio says it best: "Phil Cooke works at the intersection of faith, media, and culture, and he's pretty rare—a working producer in Hollywood with a Ph.D. in Theology." When I connected with Phil, he saw potential in me that I never saw in myself. He would challenge my work so much that it sometimes came across as harsh. (If you know Phil, you know he is being incredibly kind and supportive with a dash of grit).

I'll never forget the first time he asked me to send him a show to review. I was completely in awe that a legendary producer of Christian media production wanted to see my stuff! After all, this guy has produced programming in 70 countries around the world, including the most-watched inspirational TV programs in America—not to mention Super Bowl commercials, PBS documentaries, and much more.

He had every right to blow me to the side and move on with his life and career. However, he gave me an opportunity to step up to the plate and swing for the fences. I sent him this long and polished e-mail with a link to the show and slowly waited for a response in complete angst.

After what felt like an eternity, I saw the e-mail response come through. I could barely even open it. Remember, at this point in life, I was a kid in my early 20s with a mission to put on a TV show for college kids and young adults around the world, but I didn't have a single station committed yet.

I knew this e-mail was going to be critical to the trajectory. I opened the e-mail to find only four simple lines:

Andrew,
1. It looks like a show for jr. high kids.
2. Too many bibles and too religious.
3. Fire your audio guy.

Stick with it. You've got the goods!

Phil

I was completely crushed and elated all at the same time. Were his points valid? 100 percent! Did I do everything he suggested? Absolutely!

Year after year, I would connect with Phil digitally and in person, and he would sharpen my skills through conversation and challenge my thought process on what it meant to do "great Christian media." During a lunch together one time, I asked him why he would invite me to lunch. He responded with, "You're going places, and I just wanted to know you before everyone else does."

Do you know what that meant to me coming from a guy like Phil? Opportunity is the invitation to take your leadership to the next level. Now many years after friendship and respect had been developed, I asked Phil if he would give an endorsement to me as a producer. His words I hold with great respect and honor. "Of all the producers I know, Andrew may be the best at creating programming that connects with the next generation. His show broadcasts to nearly 200 nations. When I want to create that kind of influence, Andrew is my first call."

I truly believe because of the opportunity that Phil gave to me, I have been able to meet and work with some of the greatest professionals in Christian media. I was welcomed into the levels of leadership with the National Religious Broadcasting Association and served on the Television Committee for seven years. Every doctor has a doctor. Every leader has a leader. Opportunity makes way for opportunity.

After teaching a basic class on social media to our second-year students, Stephen had just graduated. He thought he would never touch media again, since he was about to join the U.S. Navy. Shortly after his enlistment, he was recruited to work in the media and communications area of the ship he was assigned to. His assignment early on was to cover the massive Haiti earthquake in 2010. Because of all the outages, news channels could only find and pull the media that was being sent out by Stephen and his vessel. My class gave him the basics skills he needed to produce quality media that other broadcasters could use. I gave him the opportunity, and he accepted the invitation.

After his years serving on the ship, he found himself on inactive reserve serving at the American Forces Network, a station specifically designed for United States military personnel. No matter where you were in the world, whether on a ship, Air Force base, or Army installation, AFN was there.

After getting his feet wet with his new role as master control, he met with the chaplain in charge of selecting the programming for religious media. He proposed including *Young Believer's Broadcast* in the AFN lineup. After many weeks and some intense negotiations with the Department of Defense, the vast AFN network joined 196 countries airing *Young Believer's Broadcast*! Opportunity always opens doors.

Each one of these guys played a huge role in my story, but the Oscar goes to *"Opportunity."*

When there is something in front of you that is larger than you and requires more than you, it can be a scary space. However, every half-empty glass is always equally half full. Change your perspective. Opportunity is an open door for growing your leadership.

Where does all of this leave you? There is someone in your life who has given you an opportunity to do what you're doing this very second. Thank them. People are opening doors for you right now that will lead you to the next thing you are supposed to do: respect them by paying it forward. Every time you walk through an open door of opportunity, remember to hold it for someone else coming behind you.

It is like that moment at the mall or the store where you have two sets of doors to go through, and you collide with another person going into the store at the same time. You open the door for them, and then they open the door for you. This is an opportunity. It is a gift that must be given

> **EVERY TIME YOU WALK THROUGH AN OPEN DOOR OF OPPORTUNITY, REMEMBER TO HOLD IT FOR SOMEONE ELSE COMING BEHIND YOU.**

with your great leadership. When you give another leader an opportunity, you are giving them the invitation to take their leadership to the next level. Will they mess up? Yes. Will they make mistakes on your account? Absolutely. Will they be better in their own calling because of your sacrifice? Without a doubt!

Jesus spent three years of his public ministry teaching and training the disciples to go and replicate the kingdom of God through the Church. Every active Christian believer today is a product of the opportunity Jesus gave to those disciples. You can call it whatever you want. Opportunity. Pay it forward. Build the next generation, etc.

The point is great leadership is about the opportunity that you give, not the one that you gain.

Throughout your life of leadership, you will encounter these different types of opportunities, and the power of the gift is simply recognizing what they are. I shared four stories with you that all had a foundation of opportunity, yet the present presents itself differently. Let me explain.

> **GREAT LEADERSHIP IS ABOUT THE OPPORTUNITY THAT YOU GIVE, NOT THE ONE THAT YOU GAIN.**

Opportunity of Observation

With Clayton, there was an *opportunity to observe* someone else's journey. It is amazing how much you can learn from the life of another person. You may not even know them personally, but you can observe a great deal by following them online and watching the decisions they make and the intentionality they devote to the projects they give their time to. By observing Clayton's life, I realized very early on what the skill set of making great media looked like, and as he decided to make movies, I quickly decided that movies were not for me, so I left that to him. Observation gives you a glance into a life you do not have to live. It goes deeper than simply the career stuff, too. Are you feeling the temptation to go down a negative path? Observe what has happened to marriages, careers, athletes, and highly esteemed leaders when they let their charisma overpower their character. Observe someone who has gone through a massive health and body transformation. What did it do for their life? Not only are they healthier now, but it affects their entire livelihood. They can travel easier, play with their kids, sleep better, experience less stress, and the list goes on and on. You can make great decisions for your own life simply by leaning into the opportunity to observe others.

Opportunity To Own

When I agreed to take on full production of the television show, I knew I had the opportunity to *own it*. Leadership is full of mountains to climb and barriers to jump, but you can overtake them simply by not accepting "no" and focusing on the finish line. This doesn't mean grinding your way to misery, but it means do not give up on yourself and do whatever it takes to steward your own drive. When a deadline is to be met or a challenge is up for grabs, take it! It pushes your limits as a leader and gives you the chance to prove to yourself that you can do it. By bringing in the entire show in-house, we were able to reduce costs significantly, let the students be more involved in the production of the show, and manage the workflow and the schedule in a way that wasn't a burden. At the end of the day, when an opportunity shows up at your doorstep, own it! "Own the Opportunity" is a phrase we tell younger leaders all the time. It might be an invitation to speak in a slightly larger crowd than they are used to or to oversee the inventory of the janitorial department of the local hardware store. Whatever is presented to you, own the opportunity because it is an open invitation to greater leadership impact and influence.

Opportunity of Oversight

Phil Cooke gave me the *opportunity of oversight*, a word that some would call mentorship or accountability. Regardless of what we call it, Phil's occasional oversight for me was almost like a road map over the years. One e-mail or piece of advice from him would hold me for over six months. The calls were short but potent and left me with plenty to think about. Oversight over your life is an opportunity that *everyone* should seek out. It doesn't have to be someone of fame or global influence. If they are providing value to you, that's all the influence you need. Maybe there's an established businessman in your church who you could have breakfast with once a month. Or you could have an occasional Zoom call with that teacher from high school you've kept up with and got you through to graduation. Sometimes your oversight should be professional. We should always allow doctors, Christian therapists, and qualified pastors to speak into our lives as leaders. They need to know who you are and have access to your life. It is great to have virtual mentors and people you watch from afar, but that falls more into the observation category we've already covered. These people should have access to your life in a way that can be face-to-face and frequent. Oversight is crucial because they will see your life from a different perspective than you do. Plus, we see the instructions for the oversight through an apostle all through the New Testament. The Apostle Paul spends the majority of his adult life traveling and teaching those younger in the faith. He was providing the needed oversight to the early church. Sometimes he would bring letters of congratulations and other times it would be letters full of caution or correction. Great leaders give you balanced oversight into every area they cover in your life. When you're on the ground level of life, your views can be obstructed. Trusting someone at a higher altitude gives you confidence because they see things around you and in you that you do not. It is like a track coach telling a race car driver which turn to take and what's going on around them as they fly by at 200 mph. Your life moves fast. Give yourself the opportunity of oversight, so you do not crash your life into a brick wall.

Opportunity of Offering

Finally, we have the *opportunity of offering what you have*. We know that life is full of choices, but when we see the potential in a person's life, we can give them the gift of offering an opportunity to learn, to be developed, to have a platform. This opportunity has nothing to do with you and has everything to do with the other person. However, that's the gift! It turns around and gives back to you in different ways here and there. Stephen was offered a place to learn professional skills. It did not offer him an opportunity to use athletic talent; but because he owned his opportunity, *Young Believer's Broadcast* reached a completely new audience eight years later through the American Forces Network.

When I gave Cody Graves the opportunity to host *Loud Leadership*, a podcast designed to digitally develop young adults early on in their leadership, I never knew that it would spark something in him to go on to create his own podcast that reaches a wider international audience. Cody's decision to go forward with his own platform is a gift back to me of fulfillment, knowing that I was a small part of developing something in him that would impact the world! Gift the opportunity of offering what you have to others.

Opportunity is a powerful gift that every great leader gives. Re-gift it to others to enjoy the full potential and value of the gift.

CHAPTER 23
PACE
THE POWERFUL SPEED OF SLOW

Pace promotes longevity in your leadership. A leader's attention to pace will determine the success of the mission. You've seen marathon runners on television, or maybe have even run one yourself, and you know that the number one thing people talk about to finish the race is *pace*.

It is one thing to think about pace if you're the runner, but when leaders give this gift, we become the coach. When a leader gives the gift of *pace* to a team of people, they are helping them not only win at the moment but preparing them to run their own leadership journey as well.

When I was first getting into leadership, I was excited about blasting off and conquering the unknown. I knew one speed: fast; and if I could pick a second speed, it would be faster.

My father would always tell me as I walked out of a room or finished a phone call, "Andrew, pace yourself." Of all the things he could have said as I departed into the land of mission and vision, you would think he would have said something like: "I'm proud of you," "You're the man for the job!" "Have fun!" or even the legendary, "Enjoy the journey!" Though he said all those things from time to time, the one he said most often was, "Pace yourself."

"Pace yourself? How? Why? Doesn't the world know I have things to do?" I'd think to myself.

Driven leaders typically do not do well with two topics: rest and pace. Pace can be a word that makes you feel like things are slow and boring; but in reality, it means your vision is solid and stable.

Great leaders understand that everyone is wired differently and where some love to have a to-do list of ten projects, others would be completely overwhelmed by even the thought of having more than one thing to do at a time.

Pace is what sustains the momentum in your team's efficiency and excellence. When mistakes start happening frequently, that's a sign that it is time to slow down. If culture is dragging and there's no momentum in any of the meetings or progress of the projects, it is time to speed things up.

The pace you set for your team will either propel them forward or discourage them from taking a step. The military has a saying that I believe fits here: slow is smooth, smooth is fast.

A Pace for Them

Pace must be approached seasonally, weekly, daily, and even hourly sometimes. I recommend a phenomenal book by Carey Nieuwhof: *At Your Best: How to Get Time, Energy, and Priorities Working in Your Favor*. Nieuwhof eloquently describes a framework for effective production, but I read it as a framework for pace.

How do we use this gift of pace in a practical setting around the team? For starters, we must understand that our pace as leaders will impact those we are leading. Since pace falls on a spectrum, we are constantly moving and adjusting to land at the point on the spectrum where we most need it at the time.

What can we adjust? Our re-gift to others is to recognize what their current pace is, what it needs to be, and how to get there. Here are some things that determine what the pace is...

- The speed of our speech.
- The tone of our instructions and correspondences.
- Our gait.
- Expectations for completion of assignments.
- The level of our patience.
- Our emotional response to something that catches us off guard.

When you see something in someone that needs to be developed, start with their pace. Are they on track to produce something great, or are they so stuck in their own head trying to be sure they are doing the right thing that they do not end up doing anything at all?

On the other hand, sometimes people get going so fast that if they aren't careful, they will injure their leadership gifting because they do not know the importance of good pace.

Like a 5-star athlete who injures himself and is forced to be benched for the remainder of the season, so is the leader who refuses to pace themselves in the moments that matter the most.

A Pace for Us

Pace needs to adjust through the different stages of your life. When you're young and do not have the responsibilities of marriage or family, go faster! Have the extra team hangouts, and burn the midnight oil on the passion project that just hit you at 9:00 p.m.

If you're married and starting your family with small children, face the reality that you need a different pace to survive in your life and leadership. I know guys in their sixties and even seventies who are speeding up again simply because they love what they do and have the time to do it.

Pace works for every age, and the secret is it must start with your marriage and family.

One of Amanda's uncles, who I've grown to know and love as "Tio," is a pastor in Washington state, about three hours south of Seattle.

When we first got married, I noticed that he and his wife were always taking little trips here and there. It wasn't odd to see them post about a dinner date or a matinee movie from time to time. One night while in Mexico for the holidays, I asked him, "Tio, why do you guys always take trips and random breaks here and there?" His response was annoyingly familiar, "You have to pace yourself, Mio" (which in Spanish means "little boy"). We all laughed, and then the laughter doubled down into a counseling session on ministry, marriage, and how to keep it all in balance. He began to unpack the formula he and his wife created that he calls "The 2 for 2 for 2." This may not be for everyone, but it got the point across of his purpose and what he was trying to instill in me.

- Every two weeks, go on a date.
- Every two months, getaway for one night.
- Every two years, take a vacation.

This is the secret to pace: 2 for 2 for 2.

I've already said it once in the book, but it bears repeating: your family is your first priority. Protecting your pace will provide the best of yourself to the people that matter the most. Make space and adjust the pace of your life that will show people the importance of being present for the moments that matter.

A Pace for You

The right pace will promote peace in you and in those around you. Jesus said, "Peace I leave with you, My peace I give to you" (John 14:27).

Some of the greatest doctors, therapists, and experts in the world all agree that the first thing to do when someone experiences a panic attack or crisis is to slow down their breathing. Another way to say it is to change their pace. Peace is a platform your leadership should walk firmly on daily.

Two stories come to mind from when I was young in my leadership. They both involved the same leader: my boss, my pastor, and my friend…my Dad. We would call him "Pastor Daddy" in moments of "Help, we do not know what to do." My first memory of a pace-setting pivot was a time I was leading an evening shift as the director of campus operations when a call came over the radio that a certain maintenance building had a small fire in it. Instead of responding, I reacted. I picked up the phone, trying to stay calm, and dialed Pastor Daddy.

The conversation was hard to follow on my part because I was heavy breathing so frantically that I was tripping over every single word I tried to utter. "Sir, we have a fire, and I know that everyone's ok, but I think we had some inventory from the campus services crew there, and the fire started about 10 minutes ago."

At this point, I'm just rambling over and over and over, detail after meaningless detail, for a solid two minutes. After I finally found a place to take a breath and hear his response, there was a long pause on the other side of the phone. It lasted for such a long time that I thought the call had been disconnected. Just when I was about to hang up and redial, he said, "Well, if there's a fire, we should probably put it out." The simplicity of his obvious statement made me smile, de-escalated the intensity of the moment, and gave me a clear enough head to move forward with the procedures already set forth.

Another time about three years later, I did something similar with a call around 11:00 p.m. talking about how everything started falling apart all at the same time. The network was down for the entire campus, hindering all phone systems, servers, and POS systems for opened venues. This is not what you want to hear when you have 1,000 people on the grounds trying to enjoy some free time. To make matters worse, the go-kart track had called for a medical responder for a situation that was going to require advanced medical attention, and an ambulance had been called by a group leader because they thought they heard a kid having trouble breathing, which turned out to be he was sneezing a lot from intense allergies. I was overwhelmed, and on the other end of the phone, he said, "Well, it sounds like you got your hands full, so I'll let you go so you can take care of all of that. Do not forget to pace yourself."

I again smiled, hung up the phone, and got to work. We quickly re-routed some networking traffic to a cellular solution, canceled the ambulance for "Mr. Sneezy," and re-routed the EMTs who were already on campus to the go-kart track, saving us time for what was going to require some extra help, anyway.

Changing pace will always change performance. Sometimes we just must help people get out of their feelings and double down on the facts of what they need to do to make great decisions while they are leading.

When a frustrated and frantic nine-year-old camper came into the Information Center on the last day of camp, attempting to find his lost church group, we had another chance to change the pace.

You can do that; you know? Pace can be gifted to people who aren't on your team or may not even look up to you. Your pace should carry a peace with it that is transferable to others.

CHANGING PACE WILL ALWAYS CHANGE PERFORMANCE.

After doing some searching, sure enough, we found that the church bus little Timmy was looking for was already sixty miles down the road headed home, minus one passenger. Can you imagine that meeting with that pastor and his staff on Monday morning? As the group contact began to have a meltdown on the other end of the phone, I assured him that everything was going to be fine and that we would care for him while we figured out a plan. Timmy, who started to like the idea of being "stuck at summer camp," was treated to an impromptu VIP experience by our team. We gave him extra juice and a free shirt, took him to pet the horses, and he may have even ridden a go-kart or two with extra laps on an empty track while he waited ninety minutes for his mortified group leader to return to the office. In all honesty, I think Timmy enjoyed being left behind more than he did the entire camp experience itself! We changed the pace. We took what was on the way to destruction and emotional disaster and made it a moment that he may still remember to this day.

If the goal of the leader is legacy, we must be willing to extend our energy to last longer than ever our physical leadership could. Pace will be a gift to you and the ones you give it to when you show people that their personal well-being is more important than the productivity they produce.

For the driven people who want things done yesterday, like me, let me encourage you with this challenge: slow down. There's no award for burning yourself out, and most people will not expect more from you than you do from yourself. Leading is something to enjoy, not something to complete. Bill Gates is credited with saying, "Most people overestimate what they can do in one year and underestimate what they can do in ten years."

Like a river that rushes and equally calms with stillness, so must be the pace of our leadership. Find the rhythms that work for you and accept the rest that is required if you want to deliver greatness. This marathon isn't a solo race. It is best run with people we care about and believe in. In order to pass the baton and finish strong, we must manage the pace for everyone, especially ourselves. To say it with more clarity: we must go slow if we want to last long.

WI-FI LEADERSHIP | STAYING CONNECTED TO THE PURPOSE
CONCLUSION

The life of a leader is an exhilarating one. It comes with many adventures and many trials. In the midst of the mundane or the victories of the mountain top, we must stay connected to the purpose of our leadership. I like to use the symbol of the Wi-Fi unit as a simple cue to remind me daily about the true purpose of my leadership. The first reminder is to stay connected.

CREATING A CONNECTION

Connection is the core desire of every human. To be connected means that you aren't alone and that there's someone else who is aware that you exist. When someone walks into any room for the first time, they ask two questions. Do I want to be here? Does anyone want me here? Why do they ask this? Because they long for connection.

Leadership is connecting to people and connecting them to a place on *purpose*. God the Father made our entire existence about connection. From the Garden to the Gospel, He wants a connection with His creation, and that includes *you*.

YOU

We have spent the entirety of this book talking about the important roles you will fill when you accept *the gift of leadership*. Of any profession, leaders tend to be the hardest on themselves.

Unrealistic goals are set without enough time to complete them, and the cancer of comparison eats away at our identity while we continue to experiment with being someone we were never called to be. Can I encourage you with a liberating thought? *God created you.*

The same majestic Master that threw starts into the sky, animals across the globe, and created Yellowstone's wilderness of wonder with a single word, also created you. He has declared that you are special and that you have something significant to offer the world around you.

Yes, leadership can be difficult at times; so remember to

forgo the titles and the business cards every once in a while, and just be you.

At the end of the day, with your position and potential temporarily packed away, you are only one person. You can't instantly fix everyone's issues. You can't control everything you'd secretly love to control. You are simply one person.

Like one simple circle on a never-ending canvas, your faith and relationship with Jesus should be the only thing in the infinity loop of a circular relationship. In a circle, you never know where the starting point is, or the ending.

Our relationship with Christ should model this. In a true covenant, your love for Jesus is given to Him, and instantly His unwavering love for you is received. It's like an invisible connection allowing for uploading and downloading with Jesus Christ.

Accepting His beloved identity over you will convert any wrong ambitions into wonderful adoration. You will keep your connection to leadership as you keep your connection to Christ. *Wi-Fi leadership is a simple reminder that when you stay connected to Christ, it keeps us connected to our purpose of leading people.*

I like to view this image as the symbol of a Wi-Fi unit. Every level of the semi-circle band acts as a reminder of my leadership. *Honoring the gifting, staying a giver,* and *giving gifts* are the daily road map of the leader's life.

I love this symbol because I see it almost every single day, and it reminds me of what I should do if I want to be a great leader.

> WI-FI LEADERSHIP IS A SIMPLE REMINDER THAT WHEN YOU STAY CONNECTED TO CHRIST, IT KEEPS US CONNECTED TO OUR PURPOSE OF LEADING PEOPLE.

Honor Your Gifting

In his sovereignty, God gifted this gifting of leadership to us. He entrusted us with an expression of His divine nature in the ability to speak wisdom, show integrity, and create influence in the lives of people.

We honor this gifting by protecting its sacred place in our lives. It's spiritual. It's significant. One way to ensure we are honoring our gifting is to allow the principles that power leadership to remain active in our lives daily. Principles like vision, faith, and family must remain a primary role when honoring our gifting. Why? When we honor our gifting, we honor God.

May we never take advantage of this gifting if we allow misguided motives or selfish ambition to take the place of our hearts to care for people. When we stay connected to the awareness that leadership is spiritual and significant, it makes every other level of our Wi-Fi leadership special and strong.

Stay A Giver

To be a leader is to be a servant. To be a servant means you are a giver. Over the years of leading, you will go through times where you feel that you've given too much, and now other areas of your life are suffering for it: your health, your marriage, your family, etc. While it's expected and suggested to re-align those priorities again, the one thing I'd challenge you to *not* do is stop giving. To *stay a giver* means keeping your heart in a position to continually help people. You might not be able to commit to teaching the class for the after-school program for the next six weeks, but you could call a person who needs encouragement for a six-minute phone call. To *stay a giver* means you find a way to do what you can when you can. The foundation of every great leader is their heart to help and their commitment to stay connected to the people they are leading.

Give Gifts

Leading allows every leader to see the fruit of their labor. A person that isn't confident initially but over time opens up like a blooming flower should be a gift back to you. The joy we receive when we see children open gifts on Christmas morning comes from a place of understanding that giving gifts takes work.

In order to give a gift, you have to care about the recipient, decide how you'd like to reflect that care, get the gift, and present it to the person in faith that they will receive it.

Dwayne Bohac, a former member of the Texas House of Representatives, was involved in advocating the "Merry Christmas Bill" that was signed into law in 2013. Its definition of a gift applies here: "The 'perfect gift' meets a need of the receiver but also reflects the personality of the giver."

As you lead, *give gifts*. Give the gifts that meet the need of the people you are leading. Gifts come in many shapes and sizes, and some take longer to open than others. Be patient. Let people enjoy the process of receiving their gifts. Don't be one of those people who yells out what the gift is as it's being opened. Let the recipient figure it out for themselves.

Leading will bring you the greatest joy when you remain committed to *giving gifts*.

Tie The Bow

You can start leading today! Wherever you are in the world, whatever you're feeling or facing, make a difference in someone's life today. Push them towards their purpose, and they'll help you fulfill yours, too.

Your leadership connection will constantly have you teaching people, believing in their gifts, pushing them away from distractions, upholding their choices with accountability, and giving them advice and wisdom you wish someone had given you.

The gift of leadership will meet you in many seasons of your life. Sometimes you will give, and all the time, you will gain. Jesus showed us that the greatest way to gain your life was to lay it down for a friend (John 15:13). If you choose to be a leader who demands respect and control and always wants to be the center of everyone's attention, then you will lead a very unfulfilling life. Find joy in laying your life down and giving what you have to others. It doesn't have to be in the workplace. It can be in the store or in passing on the street. You may give someone a job, or maybe just a smile. When you are giving, you are leading.

WHEN YOU ARE GIVING, YOU ARE LEADING.

My prayer is that through the pages of these principles, thoughts, lessons, scriptures, and stories, you realize the power of what great leadership can accomplish in someone's life. It is the one gift you can't buy in stores or find online. It is the gift that changes the course of a person's life and gives them a reason to hope for a better tomorrow. It is a gift that keeps giving and always provides value to a person's life, including yours. Your leadership becomes a gift when you give it away to someone else. As we tie the bow, I challenge and commission you to embrace and give *the gift of leadership* today.

YOUR LEADERSHIP BECOMES A GIFT WHEN YOU GIVE IT AWAY TO SOMEONE ELSE.

NOTES

Part I

Chapter 1

1. Oxford University Press, "Definition of principle," Lexico.com, 2021, https://www.lexico.com/en/definition/principle.

Chapter 2

2. Mancini, Will, "The Vision Frame: The Core Tool for Visionary Church Leaders," April 6, 2022, https://www.willmancini.com/the-vision-frame-the-core-tool-for-visionary-church-leaders.

3. Comer, J. M., *Ruthless Elimination of Hurry: How to Stay Emotionally Healthy and Spiritually Alive in the Chaos of the Modern World*, Crown Publishing Group, 2019.

Chapter 6

4. "Current World Population," Worldometer, April 12, 2022, https://www.worldometers.info/world-population/.

Part II

5. Maxwell, John, "Your Influence Inventory," *The John Maxwell Leadership Podcast*, April 17, 2019, https://johnmaxwellleadershippodcast.com/episodes/john-maxwell-your-influence-inventory.

6. "100 Greatest Books for Kids," Scholastic, April 20, 2022, https://www.scholastic.com/parents/family-life/parent-child/100-greatest-books-kids.html.

Chapter 11

7. The Gift of Leadership. (n.d.). Retrieved April 14, 2022, from http://www.TheGiftOfLeadership.com/dc

Chapter 13

8. Groeschel, Craig, "Learning to Lead Yourself, Part 1," *Craig Groeschel Leadership Podcast*, Life.Church, April 14, 2022,

https://www.life.church/leadershippodcast/learning-to-lead-yourself-part-1/.

Chapter 14

9. Burchfield, Peter, *Pioneering Leadership*, March 25, 2022, https://www.peterburchfield.com/.

10. Metzger, Geri K., "Vertigo," WebMD, December 12, 2020, https://www.webmd.com/brain/vertigo-symptoms-causes-treatment.

11. Coker, J. (2016, March 9). *What do you mean boundaries?* Cloud Townsend Resources. Retrieved April 14, 2022, from https://www.cloudtownsend.com/what-do-you-mean-boundaries-by-dr-henry-cloud-and-dr-john-townsend/

12. Cloud, H. (n.d.). *Coaching for your mental health and relationships*. Coaching for Your Mental Health and Relationships. Retrieved April 14, 2022, from https://www.boundaries.me/

13. Boudreaux, K. (2021, July 19). Talk With Keith | Keith Boudreaux. Retrieved April 14, 2022, from https://talkwithkeith.com/

Chapter 17

14. Maxwell, John, *Are you really leading, or are you just taking a walk?* John C. Maxwell, August 7, 2012, from https://www.johnmaxwell.com/blog/are-you-really-leading-or-are-you-just-taking-a-walk/.

ACKNOWLEDGMENTS

Throughout my life and leadership, there have been many people who've gifted me their leadership, and I would like to give words of honor to them.

To my beautiful wife, Amanda, your love and support for my gifting mean more than any words on these pages could ever describe. I love you with my life and am forever thankful for ice cream lines, "qt with qt," and the sandy beaches of Hawaii.

To our boys, Benjamin and Brayden, you've given me the opportunity of holding a role that has changed my identity forever. Being "Daddy" is one of the greatest honors of my life. You both are leaders already and give gifts to me every moment of every day.

To the late E.W. Kenyon, Damon Thompson, Mark Driscoll, Phil Cooke, and Craig Groeschel: As I've followed your teachings from a distance over the decades, they have molded me into the kingdom man I am today and have given me a model to become the leader I desire to be tomorrow. I'm forever grateful to have been *saved from the system*, and your revelations and insights have had a remarkable role in that.

To Tommy and Rachel Burchfield for the opportunity and trust, you've placed in my leadership and me for almost twenty years. It's a joy for Amanda and me to serve alongside you and build and bless His church. You are my pastors and my parents, but mostly my friends.

To my extended family from Katy and Columbus to the Rio Grande Valley and everyone in between, your acceptance of me into your worlds has been above what I could have ever prayed for. I'm humbled and honored to call you all *familia*.

To the team at New Creation Network for your excellence and efficiency in making this resource available to the world. To Chris Perry, Dave Sheets, Marcus Costantino, Vickie Deppe, and Ben Wolf, your expertise and education were invaluable.

To Travis Phillips, your energy, excitement, and encouragement to *build the dream* mean more to me than you will ever know. Thank you for helping me "build a place people love to be" in for over ten years. Your leadership is a gift to the world, and your friendship is a gift to me.

To Jonathan Eason, the array of adventures we find ourselves on is continually entertaining.

For all of the efforts and expertise you add to my day-to-day, thank you.

To Believers World Outreach Church, our heritage is strong, our future is secure, the river is still rising, and the banks will burst! Thank you for being a people that truly live + give because of Jesus.

To all the leaders mentioned in this manuscript, and the countless many who weren't, thank you for seeing the potential in me and truly being a leader worth following.

To the readers, thank you for going on a journey with me over the pages of this book. I pray my words ignited something in you and challenged you to embrace and invest in others *the gift of leadership*.

ABOUT THE AUTHOR

Andrew Burchfield is a producer with the heart of a pastor. Leading from Texas, with his wife Amanda and their two boys, he serves as the Executive Producer of *Burchfield Ministries International*, providing Bible-based resources that build and bless churches through many outreaches.

As a seasoned speaker to churches, conferences, and collegiate programs, he is admired for a spirit-led perspective that industry professionals appreciate. His influence extends to various organizations, having served on committees for the National Religious Broadcasters Association and the Department of Health for the State of Texas.

He is skilled in administration and technology to help teams create systems and solutions that promote efficiency for everyone. Having directed a summer camp for over a decade serving over half a million campers, and developed and distributed *Young Believer's Broadcast*, a Christian television show to 196 nations. Andrew excels in helping all types of teams thrive.

An avid coffee guy and skilled musician, Andrew's greatest passion is helping people produce on purpose. Connect with his life and leadership at andrewburchfield.com.

CREATION.
NETWORK

We help the Church
create &
communicate
effective media.

www.ingramcontent.com/pod-product-compliance
Lightning Source LLC
Chambersburg PA
CBHW030258100526
44590CB00012B/441